avenue
media solutions

Keep making a difference!
Best wishes,
Neil.

Keep up the
good work !
J. m...

Published by Avenue Media Solutions www.AvenueMediaSolutions.com

Social work is one of the most misunderstood and difficult professions there is. It can be physically and emotionally draining, but it is also one of the most rewarding professions there is. Social work has been put under immense pressure, hit hard by years of austerity and forgotten when it comes to key/frontline workers in the coronavirus pandemic. In a world of increasing complexity and demands, where human connections and interactions are decreasing, social workers will be needed and valued more than ever before. Armed with this book you won't just survive social work, but thrive in it too.

Emma Lewell-Buck MP (former social worker), Member of Parliament for South Shields

Ten chapters packed full of key strategies, guidance, insight and support that all social work students will find essential reading as they progress through their studies and into practice. SCRATCH and BEYOND are surely the new frameworks for students to pop into their growing toolkits! The language is easy to read and relatable, the content refreshing as it acknowledges the importance of reflective practice in an increasingly pressurized role – while recognizing that it is possible to not only survive, but also thrive in social work today! At the Student Social Work Hub we believe that's what everyone should be aiming for.

The Student Social Work Hub, https://thestudentsocialworkhub.wordpress.com

This is a must-read for social workers and their employers. Social work is widely understood to be one of the most stressful jobs in the UK and beyond, meaning there is a clear need for books that outline the problem as well as methods for individuals, management and organizations to address the problem. This book does each of these things from an expert-informed and research-based perspective. I would recommend that social work professionals and employers read this book and use the stress management skills suggested for the betterment of individual well-being, which will subsequently improve outcomes for service users.

Dr Jermaine M. Ravalier, Bath Spa University

This welcome book is about more than survival, important though that is. It invites us to go beyond 'good enough' into a Nietzschean affirmation, a 'saying yes' to life and to social work, while remaining rooted in a realism that transcends both a deadening negativity on the one hand and a rose-tinted optimism on the other. And, as the authors so rightly remind us throughout, it is crucial that we do this collectively. So, buy, share, read, discuss this book together, with your team or at your trade union or professional association branch. Survive, and thrive, in solidarity!

Guy Shennan, The Solution-Focused Collective www.guyshennan.com

An entirely readable and timely reminder of all we learned in our social work training, together with some contemporary critical thinking around why our work can be even more challenging in these difficult times, with practical advice on what needs to happen to help us all to thrive (not just survive!). Every social worker, at any stage in their career, should have a copy close to hand to dip into regularly and to remind us what a complex, but wonderfully interesting and rewarding job social work is!

Lien Watts, Head of Advice and Representation, British Association of Social Workers

How to Survive in Social Work

By

Neil Thompson and John McGowan

With a Foreword by Ruth Allen, An Afterword by
David N. Jones and illustrations by Harry Venning

Contents

About the authors

Dr Neil Thompson is an independent writer, educator and adviser. He has held full or honorary professorships at four UK universities and has been a speaker at seminars and conferences in the UK, Ireland, Italy, Spain, Portugal, Greece, the Netherlands, Norway, the Czech Republic, Turkey, Hong Kong, India, Canada, the United States and Australia. He has over 300 publications to his name, including several best-selling textbooks. His recent publications include *The Values-based Practice Manual* (with Bernard Moss) and *The Problem Solver's Practice Manual* (both published by Avenue Media Solutions).

He is also the programme director for the Avenue Professional Development Programme, an online learning community based in principles of self-directed learning and geared towards developing critically reflective practice. Recent work involves the development of two further online learning programmes, *Survive in Social Work* and *The Social Work Finishing School*, the latter being especially designed for final-year students, newly qualified workers and experienced practitioners and managers wanting a refresher and to be re-energized.

He is a partner in the *humansolutions* Health & Well-being Portal (www.humansolutions.org.uk) which was set up to help pressurized individuals to stay fit and healthy. He also acts as a consultant to CaringBusinessBuilder, a service geared towards supporting self-employed professionals to manage their businesses effectively (www.CaringBusinessBuilder.com).

His website and Learning Zone, with free learning resources, are at www.NeilThompson.info.

John McGowan *MSc, BA, DipSW* is a social worker and a British trade unionist who is the current General Secretary of the Social Workers Union. He initially served on the UK Council for the British Association of Social Workers as a non-Executive Director between 2008 and 2012 before moving to the post of Vice President of the Social Workers Union 2012 to 2016. He also served on the Scottish Association of Social Workers Executive Committee 2004 to 2014 and latterly as its Depute Convenor. John was elected as General Secretary of the Social Workers Union in 2016 for a 5-year period. More recently, he has been active with the

General Federation of Trade Unions (290,000 members) and presently he sits on their National Executive Committee.

John is also an associate lecturer with the Open University and teaches regularly on the widening participation programme, a post that he has been doing with access courses since 2004. John is also the Programme Tutor for the Open University Social Work Degree programme in Scotland. Previously he served as an elected member of the Open University's governing body, the UK Council.

Since qualifying as a social worker in the 1990s. John has predominately worked in the field of Children and Families, Fostering and Adoption and as a training officer/ practice teacher. He has worked in a variety of settings, working for local authorities as well as the third sector. He was formerly an independent panel chair of the Adolescent and Children's Trust.

John is proud of his working-class upbringing in the Muirhouse housing estate in Edinburgh, which is regarded as one of the most deprived areas in Scotland. His early experiences of social work were through his family, as his parents were active foster carers in Edinburgh, fostering over 100 children in total.

Acknowledgements

We would like to express our heartfelt thanks to Dr Ruth Allen for her Foreword and David N. Jones for his Afterword. We are fortunate to have such eminent and highly respected social work professionals add their weight to the important messages we are making in this book.

We would also like to thank our colleagues in BASW and SWU for their ongoing support in relation not only to this book, but also to our work more broadly in our shared endeavour of supporting social workers and promoting the value of social work.

We are grateful to the people who kindly provided endorsements to confirm the value of the book and highlight the positive difference we very much hope it will be able to make.

Neil would like to acknowledge the role of Dr Sue Thompson who plays such an important part in so many aspects of his work and their daughter, Anna, who, as always, has been unstinting in her practical support.

John would like to thank Deirdre Henderson and their two children for so many things that, if they were all listed, the Acknowledgements would need to be ordered as a separate supplement.

Last, but not least, we would like to thank Harry Venning for his marvellous illustrations. How impoverished the British social work scene would be without his superb artwork and rich sense of humour! Harry is an award-winning cartoonist, illustrator and comedy writer. A weekly contributor to THE GUARDIAN with the CLARE IN THE COMMUNITY strip, his work has also appeared in THE MAIL ON SUNDAY, SUNDAY TELEGRAPH, INDEPENDENT, SUNDAY TIMES, THE STAGE and RADIO TIMES, as well as publications in Canada, Switzerland, South Africa and New Zealand – plus books, lots of books. Harry is also a member of the exclusive CARTOONIST CLUB OF GREAT BRITAIN, with work displayed in the Cartoon Museum, London. Find out more about his work at: http://www.harryvenning.co.uk/.

Preface

For quite some time now we have been seeing some significant changes in the world of work, and not always positive ones. What one generation of workers knew as the norm of a stable job on a permanent basis, for the next generation has evolved into much greater variety in terms of what they can expect in a work context. Of course, permanent jobs still exist, but alongside these we have seen the growth of temporary contracts, a significant increase in self-employment (the 'gig economy') and zero hours contracts, making work a much more uncertain part of people's lives, potentially creating significantly more anxiety and the problems such increased anxiety can cause.

We have also seen a philosophy of 'more for less' develop as part of a neoliberal approach to economy and society, bringing about significantly higher levels of pressure and thus a higher chance of people experiencing health-affecting stress. This has (not coincidentally) accompanied a declining level of power and influence for trade unions.

Rapid and accelerating developments in technology have made many former jobs unnecessary and radically transformed others, with some winners and many losers. As Friedman (2014) explains:

> Today things are different. Our work is infinitely more complex. We rarely need employees to simply do routine, repetitive tasks. – we also need them to collaborate, plan, and innovate. Building a thriving organization in the current economy demands a great deal more than efficiency. It requires an environment that harnesses intelligence, creativity, and interpersonal skill.
>
> (p. xv)

These changes apply across the world of work as a whole and social work has not been in any way an exception. In particular, the adoption of neoliberal thinking at a political level has filtered down to social work policy and practice at the community and family level, bringing additional pressures, dilemmas and tensions.

By its very nature, social work is a demanding occupation. It involves working with people who are facing major life challenges, often in situations where the resources available to them are limited. Demand is infinite while supply is finite; the general public, fuelled by the distortions of the media, often have a very limited grasp of what we do or its value, there can be conflict with other professionals and we are regularly coming face to face with pain, suffering, distress, grief, trauma and abuse, often with such intensity that it can be quite challenging for us to deal with our own emotions. Added to this is the fact that the quality of management and leadership for social workers is highly variable, ranging from some examples of excellence, demonstrating outstanding ability and commitment, to levels of practice that are frankly just not good enough.

Anyone who enters the world of social work therefore needs to be well prepared for rising to the many challenges involved and, ideally, be the sort of person who relishes such challenges. The job itself is demanding and the context in which we do it has become harder and harder over the years. It is therefore no surprise that both authors regularly come across people – very competent and talented people – who are struggling to cope with the demands of what at times can feel like an impossible job.

That is where this book comes in. We have written it to formally acknowledge the immense difficulty in just getting through the day and to make it clear that struggling to deal with the huge demands in difficult circumstances is nothing to be ashamed of. In fact, it is steadily becoming the norm for a large number of people. It is also our aim, in putting this text together, to offer help in terms of how to tackle the challenges we face. There are ways and means of coping, and it is our firm belief that the very nature of social work as an enterprise geared towards problem solving and empowerment places us in a strong position to not only survive, but also to thrive – to be in a position to make a positive difference despite all the obstacles we face and the enormity of the task.

What we want to aim for is what Costello (2020) describes in the following terms:

> We thrive when the physical, intellectual, emotional, relational, and spiritual domains of what it is to be human are given the opportunity to be expressed.

(p. 16, emphasis in the original)

Social work, with its roots in drawing on the positives of authentic human connection, put us in a strong position to do precisely that if we are first able to rise to the challenges of surviving in a fairly hostile neoliberal climate.

Foreword

Social workers across the UK deserve to thrive and be well supported and respected in their hugely valuable work – helping people progress in their lives and promoting rights and well-being. This is what it should mean to be a social work professional in the 21st century. I hope all current and trainee social workers hold their own version of this as an unshakeable vision for themselves and their colleagues.

These ideas drive what we do in the British Association of Social Workers, working with our partner, the Social Workers Union. This book is a tremendously important, accessible and timely contribution to help our whole social work community take forward our vision of a thriving, confident profession.

For too long, many social workers have reported that their organizational working conditions hinder rather than facilitate their work – particularly in statutory services where social workers undertake complex, life-changing practice every day. Individual narratives from practitioners are backed up by the findings of systematic workforce research, as summarized in the book. Too often social workers describe unfeasible demands, excessive workloads, poor management approaches, a lack of professional control and autonomy and inadequate professional and career development support. They also too often describe feeling that they don't have the individual and collective power to change their situation.

As professionals, we need to find and use our ideas, voice, power and skills to change this narrative – individually, with colleagues and as a collective force. This includes through the solidarity of being part of professional networks, the professional association and trade union.

This incredibly timely book contextualizes current social workers' experiences in the impact of the post-2008 financial crash, austerity and funding cuts. This has had many negative impacts on the quality and quantity of services, and on the experience of social workers and other public professionals. Not least of these is the widening of distressing gaps between what social workers want and know they should be able to do to be helpful and to protect people's rights and the shrunken material and emotional resources often available.

But the book also offers a longer arc of social work history, locating the structural roots of stressful working conditions in previous decades from when neoliberal social, political and economic thinking shaped welfare policy, public sector reorganizations, privatization and disinvestment. Many organizational cultures have been shaped over these years by transactional 'managerialism' that, at its worst, dehumanizes and strips meaning from the deeply human, relationship-based and life-enhancing practices that should be at the heart of social work. Time and space for reflection, professional critical analysis and learning have been devalued too often, contributing further to endemic cultures of harmful stress in many social work organizations.

In a clear, confident and compassionate style, the authors show this is not an inevitable state of affairs. The current situation is challenging, but everyone involved in social work – practitioners, supervisors, managers, leaders, educators, researchers – can make a difference. Current progress by good employers and other organizations is recognized, and the helpful, balanced summary of research provides an insight to what we already know about the challenges and the solutions.

This book provides an excellent exposition of how every social worker can take personal, professional and collective action – and not be alone. It clearly summarizes key areas of theory and knowledge that will help social workers contextualize and understand their situations, why they may feel the way they do about work, and overcome feelings of powerlessness to connect and stay connected with their motivation and agency, and with each other.

It explores and encourages personal self-care, self-awareness, personal honesty and true resilience while also encouraging a clearer understanding and integration of local and wider structural factors at play – such as bullying, inequality, discrimination or unacceptable workloads in their organization and wider political, economic and social forces. To paraphrase a quote from German sociologist, Ulrich Beck, the book clarifies that we can't simply seek individual 'biographic' solutions to 'structural contradictions'.

The book is grounded in the legal and ethical responsibilities of employing organizations towards their staff. Harmful stress in a legal sense is not something any employer can afford to ignore. Poor working conditions and unfeasible workloads affect productivity, morale, workforce stability, the quality of services, citizen experience – and lead to legal challenge. This book should be a positive encouragement to managers, organizational leaders and others to work collaboratively and take their lead from practitioners and from their professional knowledge and experience of doing social work, and to work with organizations representing social workers professionally and through trade unions.

Dr Ruth Allen
Chief Executive Officer
British Association of Social Workers

Introduction

Social work is a key part of making our society a humane and caring society. It bypasses the common tendency to superficially 'look on the bright side' as if pain and suffering either do not exist or are too unimportant to be worthy of sustained attention. As such, it is rooted in *realism* in the sense that we see the glass as both half empty and half full. We are not pessimists who see only the negatives in life, nor are we naïve optimists who want to pretend the sun is always shining.

The highly influential philosopher, Friedrich Nietzsche (1844-1900), emphasized the importance of affirming life, but he also warned against turning our backs on the less positive sides of life. More recently, this ethos has been shared by Davies (2012) who argues that it is important to recognize the value and meaning of emotional discontent. We shall return later to his work on the importance of suffering, but for now we want simply to highlight realism, as we are using the term here, as one of the important foundations of social work. It is this realism that brings not only challenges, but also potential rewards and enrichment. The challenges are what we need to survive, and the rewards and enrichment are what enable us to thrive.

Moving from surviving to thriving is what this book is all about. We shall be focusing on not only how we manage to withstand the immense pressures of modern-day social work, but also how to make the most of the opportunities so that we can flourish.

Getting up to SCRATCH and BEYOND

To get up to scratch means to achieve an acceptable standard. It therefore serves well as an analogy for surviving – managing to do at least the bare minimum to get by. We are drawing on this analogy to encapsulate our approach to how to survive in social work by using it as an explanatory framework:

> **S**olidarity – We are in this together; the more we pull together and support one another, the stronger a position we will be in. While this may seem obvious, unfortunately, what happens very often when people are under

considerable pressure is that they retreat into what they see as the safety of their own personal 'security bubble'. The reality is that we are safer when we pull together, rather than pull apart.

Caring for yourself – There is a risk of being traumatized and/or burnt out by the pressures we face in such a challenging occupation as social work. Self-care is therefore essential. As we shall be emphasizing, we will be in a weak position to care for others if we are not caring for ourselves. Sadly, though, despite this importance, a lack of self-care is not at all uncommon in social work.

Reaffirming professionalism – In the UK we have a longstanding tradition of playing down the significance of professionalism and the important knowledge, skills and values on which it is based. This is very unfortunate, as taking pride in our professionalism and the highly important contribution we make to society and social welfare is a valuable source of motivation to sustain us through the enormous difficulties we face.

Avoiding stress While pressure is an inevitable part of social work, stress (in the sense of harmful levels of pressure) is not inevitable. One of the dangers is allowing stress to become 'normalized' – that is, so common that it is assumed to be intrinsic to our work. Stress, as we shall see, is a sign that there is something wrong that needs to be addressed. Accepting it as 'par for the course' masks the fact that it can be avoided if handled properly.

Theory driven – There is a huge knowledge base that we can draw on to make sense of working life and how it affects us psychologically and socially. Stress can generate a sense of powerlessness and helplessness, but drawing on relevant theory – especially empowerment theory – enables us to have hope that steps can be taken to address the causes of excessive pressure and develop strategies for coping as effectively as we can.

Challenging – This involves being assertive and not accepting harmful working practices that put our health and well-being at risk. This brings us back to solidarity and the need for us to work together – challenging collectively is clearly going to be far more effective than each individual trying to do it alone. As the saying goes, hang together or hang alone. Constructive challenging therefore has an important role to play.

Holistic approach – The traditional approach to stress and workplace challenges more broadly has tended to be psychologically based and therefore with a strong individualistic focus. We view this as unhelpful, as it encourages an 'if you are stressed, it is your own fault' mentality. The holistic approach we are using therefore seeks to incorporate both micro and macro factors, reflecting how important the wider context is.

We hope that this acronym will help you to see where we are coming from when it comes to surviving in social work. There will always be pressures, demands and challenges – such is the nature of social work – but there will always also be ways of responding to these. As one of the present authors (Neil) has put it before:

For me, this is what social work is all about: making the best of difficult situations while also addressing those factors that are making it difficult – rather than allowing the problems we encounter to grind us down. The greater the problems we face, the greater the heart we need – and the more we need to pull together and support one another in taking forward what we believe in.

(Thompson, 2020a, p. 190)

However, this book is not just about surviving; we also need to consider what is involved in thriving. For this we have BEYOND, another acronym, another framework for distilling some of the key issues we need to be aware of – and engage with – if thriving is to stand any chance of being a reality in such highly pressurized circumstances:

Best practice – 'Satisficing' is the technical term for aiming simply for 'good enough', rather than going for the best outcomes possible. The term is made up of *satis*factory and sacri*ficing*. Once we reach a satisfactory level, we sacrifice doing even better. One of the features of professionalism is that we aim for optimal results, best practice, rather than satisfactory practice. Being committed to best practice will stand us in good stead for thriving.

Empowerment – If we are to be serious about thriving, not just surviving, then we need to do more than pay lip service to the concept of empowerment. It is about making sure that our actions not only contribute to the empowerment of others, but also do not play a part in disempowering ourselves. Power is a key theme in social life in general and in social work in particular. Making sure that it is being used positively and ethically is therefore essential.

Yes saying – This does not mean saying yes to too much work! It is a deeper matter than that. The philosopher, Friedrich Nietzsche, whose work we mentioned earlier, distinguished between yes-saying and nay-saying attitudes to life. The former is positive and affirming, while the latter is negative and self-defeating. As we shall see, excessive pressure tends to generate negativity, defeatism and cynicism. These have no place in any genuine commitment to thriving.

One for all and all for one – We have already emphasized the importance of solidarity for surviving, but it is also essential for thriving. Effective teamwork, skilled partnership working and a collective approach to challenges faced are all core elements of getting the best results. Giving and receiving support, making sure we communicate effectively and being empathic towards others are not optional extras if thriving is to be our aim.

Neverending learning – Sadly, many people see continuous professional development as a bureaucratic matter of keeping professional registration bodies off their back. If we are genuinely to thrive, we need to get beyond that and embrace the idea that we need to be well tuned in to learning opportunities and prepared to take advantage of them as far as possible. We need to move from a passive approach to learning to a more active, self-directed one.

Determination to succeed – Resilience is understandably an important concept in social work (albeit misused at times), and it is especially important when it comes to being determined to succeed. This is not about blind ambition, but rather a recognition that thriving depends in large part on being able to press on and do our best, despite the many discouragements, obstacles and setbacks we are likely to face, to bounce back when we encounter adversity.

How getting up to SCRATCH and BEYOND plays out in practice should become much clearer in the pages that follow. But, for now, it should give you a basis of understanding that we will be building on. So, please bear these ideas in mind, not only as you make your way through the book, but also as you wrestle with the very real challenges of surviving and thriving in social work.

Chapter 1: Surviving in Context

Introduction

As we have already discussed in the Preface, it is important to understand the broader context of working life in this day and age if we are to avoid having too narrow and misleading a perspective. It is essential that we develop a more holistic picture that explores the situation from a broad range of angles. This, of course, involves considering both micro and macro elements, something we shall do in much fuller detail in Chapter 3.

The focus in this chapter is on broad sociopolitical trends that have, for quite some time now, been serving to increase pressures on the workforce in general and the social work workforce in particular. It is understandable that social workers will see the workplace situation through their own eyes and therefore base their understanding on what they are hearing, seeing and engaging in on a daily basis. We have no reason to doubt the validity of those perceptions, of course, but we do recognize that it can be helpful to locate those direct experiences in a wider context so that we have a fuller picture of what is happening and a stronger basis for addressing the problems and threats involved.

There is no single reason for the various challenges that are currently facing us, and so no simple single solution. Consequently, a key part of what we are trying to achieve in this chapter is to develop an appreciation of the complex forces that are operating in and around the modern workplace. By grasping the significance of those forces, we are better placed to: (i) explore potential solutions to the problems involved (solutions that do not pathologize the individual as part of a process of victim blaming – see Chapter 3); and (ii) not fall into the trap of self-blame by assuming that, if we are struggling, then that must be our own fault (see Chapter 10).

Space does not permit a full and detailed analysis of all of the reasons for the current difficulties in the workplace, and so we are going to be more realistic in our ambitions by focusing on a smaller number of what we regard as the most salient ones. We begin by considering a political philosophy that has proven to be extremely influential and extremely problematic.

Neoliberalism

If we are to have anything approaching an adequate understanding of today's workplace challenges, we need to consider the wider political context, particularly in terms of the dominance of neoliberal thinking in recent decades. Neoliberalism, as we noted earlier, places considerable emphasis on market forces. The 'liberal' element of the term is what this refers to – that is, economic liberalism or a laissez-faire approach based on the idea that the economy will flourish if restrictions on it are kept to a minimum. It involves relying on the market to regulate the economy and thus, in some ways, society. It is assumed that the market will find its own optimal level. For example, if a product is in short supply, its price will go up. As a product becomes more freely available, its price will go down. It is assumed, in neoliberal thinking, that there should be no interference in the market unless absolutely necessary.

The 'neo' element of neoliberalism refers in part to how there has been in recent decades a resurgence of this type of thinking. The concept dates to far beyond the days of Thatcherism (and Reaganism in the USA), but the success of these two political figures in promoting neoliberal thinking and practices has played a key role in shaping modern political and economic thinking and organization.

Neoliberalism has had a number of significant effects in shaping modern society. Here we are going to consider three in particular. First there is the significance of increasing inequality (Atkinson, 2018), a phenomenon that, of course, has significant consequences for social work, in so far as it is those sectors of society who form the majority of our clientele who are likely to be most adversely affected by it.

Increasing inequality

There is now considerable evidence to support the idea that the gap between the poorest in society and the richest is growing at a considerable and alarming rate. This inequality is not simply a matter of economics. It has much wider consequences in terms of social life. As Dorling (2019, p. 1) puts it: 'Growing income and wealth inequality is recognised as the greatest social threat of our times'. In an earlier work, he explains this more fully:

> Recent scientific evidence of many kinds makes it increasingly clear that great inequality in modern societies is damaging: damaging to human abilities, performance and happiness. We can now see that most of the differences in outcomes between rich and poor, whether in measures of IQ, health, violence or educational attainment, which are so often used to justify elitism, hierarchy and social exclusion, are in fact caused by social status differentiation itself. That is why more hierarchical societies with bigger income differences between rich and poor have so many more of almost all the health and social problems which tend to be more common lower down the social ladder.
>
> (Dorling, 2011, p. xvi)

Many examples are to be found in the work of Wilkinson and Pickett (2010, 2019) which provides a strong evidence base to highlight the extent to which inequality contributes to greater levels of mental health problems, alcohol- and drug-related problems and other social ills. The greater the extent of economic inequality, the greater the extent and severity of social problems (Thompson, 2017a), and consequently further pressures on the citizens we serve, particularly those in the more disadvantaged and vulnerable sectors of society.

As Wilkinson and Pickett (2010) explain:

> It is a remarkable paradox that, at the pinnacle of human material and technical achievement, we find ourselves anxiety-ridden, prone to depression, worried about how others see us, unsure of our friendships, driven to consume and with little or no community life. Lacking the relaxed social contact and emotional satisfaction we all need, we seek comfort in over-eating, obsessive shopping and spending, or become prey to excessive alcohol, psychoactive medicines and illegal drugs.
> How is it that we have created so much mental and emotional suffering despite levels of wealth and comfort unprecedented in human history?
>
> (p. 3)

Deregulation

The second major effect of neoliberalism has been an emphasis on deregulation. If interference in the market is to be kept to a minimum, then it follows that any government regulation of business should also be kept to a minimum.

This is often expressed as a commitment to 'getting rid of red tape'. This is a clever ideological appeal to make life more streamlined and less hemmed in by bureaucracy. Who would not want that?

However, a more critical analysis of the concept reveals that it is not as benign as it initially appears. Closer examination reveals that what are targeted for removal are not obstacles to efficiency as such, but, rather, obstacles to maximum profitability. 'Getting rid of red tape' can therefore be understood as a euphemism for three worrying and problematic developments. It can be seen as amounting to undermining:

1. *Workers' rights* Progress made in the development of rights and protections is at risk because of neoliberal thinking which strongly supports the interests of the power elite at the expense of ordinary working people. An example of this would be health and safety provisions. Arguably, paying attention to health and safety measures will benefit a business in the long run. However, many such measure involve costs (providing protective equipment, for example), and will therefore generally be seen as a bind, rather than a boon.

2. *Consumer protection* Gains made in promoting the rights of consumers are also at risk to the extent that they can be seen to reduce profits by increasing costs. Much legislation, including that emanating from the European Union, has focused on protecting consumers from unscrupulous business practices (for example, selling substandard goods and refusing to offer a refund). As with health and safety, consumer protection is arguably a good thing for business as satisfied customers are much more likely to come back for more in due course, but, despite this, consumer protections are often perceived as a drain on profitability.

3. *Environmental protection measures* These too are under threat where they have an adverse effect on profitability. Donald Trump's total refusal to engage with programmes intended to safeguard our habitat is a prime example of the tendency to put profit before environmental sustainability. Less extreme examples are very easy to find in the UK too and elsewhere around the world. The idea that investing in environmental protection is precisely that – an investment – has yet to achieve mainstream acceptance in the corridors of power. Failing to protect our habitat is going to do more damage to the economy than providing the funding necessary for environmental protection – indeed, it could be argued that such investment will actually serve to stimulate the economy.

What seems superficially like a good idea (reducing waste and unnecessary bureaucracy) can therefore be understood more critically as a tilting of the balance in favour of the wealthiest elements of society, thereby feeding further inequality and the associated problems.

Government regulation exists for a reason, or a set of reasons, with protection from harm and exploitation serving as a unifying theme. The rhetoric of deregulation therefore needs to be questioned, as what seems initially like a sensible idea reveals more sinister motives below the surface, motives that are enshrined within neoliberalism.

Rolling back the state

The third element is the shrinking of the state and the role of democratically elected governments. A key aspect of neoliberalism is an emphasis on reducing the role of public bodies in social life. Consequently, what we have seen in recent decades as a result of neoliberal thinking is the undermining of the welfare state to the point where it is now increasingly viewed as a residual state. The term 'residual' is used to refer to a conception of the state as a minimal provider of a safety net. This has the effect of reducing investment in public services, again with a greater emphasis on a reliance on the market. This is the rationale behind the strong emphasis on privatization.

A welfare state is one that is based on the assumption that governments – national and local – have a key role to play in securing and safeguarding citizens' welfare. A residual state, by contrast, is one that reduces the role of government to the bare minimum, playing largely a regulatory role, leaving citizen welfare to individuals, families and communities (hence the short-lived popularity of the idealistic notion of 'the big society' put forward in David Cameron's day). While there is certainly much more that could be done to strengthen individual, family and community support, there can be few people working in social work who do not recognize that what is currently available is in any sense adequate. 'Rolling back the state' therefore needs to be understood as a mechanism that shifts funding away from public services at the expense of those people who rely heavily on those services. And, of course, the wealthier people are, the less they tend to rely on public services (consider private health care, private education and so on), which means that the adverse effects of a lower level of investment in public services is disproportionately felt by the poorest sectors of society.

It is interesting to note that the Covid-19 crisis quickly exposed a tension between protection of the economy and the protection of the population. We mean this in the sense that there were strong pressures to end lockdown restrictions as soon as possible for the sake of the economy (getting people back to work, getting the shops, pubs, cafés and restaurants open again, and so on), even though this would increase the risk of infection and, for some people, death.

The appearance of heavily armed protesters in the United States expressing strongly their objection to protective measures geared towards preventing infection highlights how fervent an objection to governmental involvement in private life can be. The instances of store assistants being shot because they asked customers to wear a mask further exemplify the extremes to which this thinking can be taken.

The expression of such beliefs tends to be less vehement and generally more subtle, but it would be a mistake to naively assume that such sentiments are not part of UK culture, such is the dominance of neoliberal thinking.

Despite this dominance, there are significant flaws in the logic underpinning it. In particular it is worth focusing on three. First, there is the notion of trickle-down economics. This refers to the idea that, the more wealthy a country becomes, the better it will be for everybody, because the wealth generated will 'trickle down' from the richest elements of society to the poorest. Of course, this does not happen. What we have seen is the classic scenario that the rich get richer while the poor get poorer, as reflected in Dorling's extensive work highlighting the adverse effects of inequality (Dorling, 2018; 2019). Monbiot (2016) makes an important point when he argues that:

> In reality, the free market is a political construction ... Far from being a neutral forum, the market is dominated by powerful agents – corporations and oligarchs – who use their position to demand special treatment: contracts, handouts, tax breaks, treaties, the crushing of resistance and other political favours. They extend their power beyond their trading relationships through their ownership of the media and their funding and control of political parties.
>
> (pp. 3-4)

Second there is the assumed 'wisdom' of the market. Allowing social policies to be determined by impersonal market forces can be seen as far from wise. The complexity of social policy is such that assuming that the effects of market forces will be sufficient to generate optimal outcomes is both naïve and dangerous. Billig (2013, p. 138) captures this point well when he comments on the folly of ascribing motives to: 'these so-called "objective entities", making them act as if they were human'. He goes on to explain:

> For example, we can read about market forces that dictate/demand/forbid, as if these forces spring to life to perform the human actions of dictating, demanding and forbidding. Moreover, these strange forces seem to crowd out actual people and their actions. The result is that the humans, who have power over others through their trading and owning, become invisible. In their place, abstract economic forces take on the role of quasi-humans, demanding obeisance from the real humans.

The use of market forces language therefore serves to camouflage the actions (and vested interests) of powerful players in the economy and society. In a sense, it can be seen as a form of modern feudalism, in the sense that the lords and barons power elite of the feudal era have been replaced by market forces (read billionaires) and the serfs and vassals by consumers who have been taught that consumption is the path to happiness (in the same way that feudal subjects were taught that their lowly place was a reflection of the natural order).

Third, Chang (2010) argues that the option of a free market unfettered by state involvement is a myth. As Thompson (2017a) explains:

> Chang points out that there are restrictions on what can be traded (arms, for example), certain products have to be licensed (medicines, for example) and various other ways in which we can see that the market is not as free as its proponents make out. They also tend to neglect the huge government subsidies that are invested in private companies – for example, the research underpinning medication development that the pharmaceutical industry subsequently profits from.
>
> (p. 7)

Clearly, then, neoliberalism is highly ideological, presenting its tenets as 'the logic of the market', while masking the power imbalances and forms of political, economic and social exploitation that underpin it.

Equating economy and society

Our third concern is the questionable assumption that the economy and society can be equated, as if society is just a reflection or side effect of the economy. While it is fully accepted that modern society relies on an effective economy, to put all our eggs in the basket of the economy is a dangerous step to take. There are many aspects of society worthy of being paid attention in their own right, separate from the economy. For example, the Covid-19 crisis that began to have major effects early in 2020 highlighted the importance of addressing social need, even though this had significant economic implications in terms of public spending and potential or actual budget deficits.

Neoliberalism and trade unionism

A further aspect of neoliberalism is the weakening of trade unionism following Margaret Thatcher's concerted efforts to undermine the power of organized labour to challenge government policy or other aspects of how the ruling elite benefit from inequality in society. There were deliberate attempts to switch the balance of power from workers to managers and wider organizational stakeholders. This has resulted in a weakening of worker protections and given managers and others a much stronger hand to play in negotiations.

Reflective of this is the often-heard phrase in some quarters of 'the manager's right to manage'. This represents an adversarial approach to manager-worker relations. American billionaire Warren Buffett is famous for, among other things, saying that there is indeed a class war and his class (the extremely wealthy) are winning the war. And, of course, he is right.

Contrast this with the human resources philosophy of a manager-worker partnership. This thinking has been significant in developing the modern emphasis on workplace well-being. It is based on the recognition that all parties will benefit from having a less adversarial approach and more of a mutually beneficial partnership approach to working life.

However, this philosophy can turn out to be tokenistic if it is not fully understood in the context of partnership. If working relations are seen as a war to be won, rather than as a potentially mutually beneficial working arrangement, then there is a high price to pay for all involved (Thompson, 2013a).

However, it is not simply about workers versus managers in the traditional sense; it is much broader than this. It reflects wider sociopolitical factors, such as the tension between labour and capital more broadly, rather than just specifically within particular work sites. This, in turn, is part of a broader picture of the tension and conflict of interest between the populace and the power elite – that is, the general public and those who are in privileged positions of power because of wealth, accidents of birth associated with aristocracy or other such aspects of the social structure.

Unions are, by their very nature, organizations that unify, that bring people together to promote shared interests. Historically, a major part of this has been preventing unscrupulous employers from imposing inadequate, exploitative levels of pay; unhelpful, dangerous or harmful working systems and practices; unrealistic workload expectations; or other such actions or omissions that are likely to have a detrimental effect on all or sectors of the workforce. There is therefore a strong protective element to trade unionism. It does not take too much of a leap of logic to recognize that trade unionism would be seen as a threat to the interests of those in our society who seek to maximize their wealth and power at the expense of ordinary people.

It was not, therefore, a simple accident of history that Margaret Thatcher's government did so much to reduce union (and thus worker) power. However, despite her best efforts, trade unionism has continued to be a powerful and valuable force for good in modern society, albeit with a lower level of influence than was previously the case. This is a major factor in terms of how and why the current overpressurized workplace has emerged. Neoliberalism, while disingenuously presenting itself as of benefit to everyone, has continued to serve the interests of the power elite at the expense of ordinary people. Consequently, if we wish to develop an adequate understanding of today's major workplace challenges, we need to take account of how the weakening of trade union protections has allowed such worker-unfriendly workplaces to emerge and become the norm in so many places.

The renowned sociologist Ulrich Beck uses the emphasis on flexibility as an example of the subtle (and sometimes not-so-subtle) shifts in the balance of power, influence and rights:

> Calls are made everywhere for greater 'flexibility' – or, in other words, that employers should be able to fire employees with less difficulty. Flexibility also means a redistribution of risks away from the state and the economy towards the individual. The jobs on offer become short-term and easily terminable (i.e. 'renewable').

> (2000, p. 3)

This is not to say that flexible approaches to working life never bring advantages to workers, but it does need to recognize that one person's (or corporation's) flexibility is another person's insecurity and potential contributor to stress.

Trade unionism has an important role to play in resisting unfair and exploitative working practices and conditions, despite the fact that, unfortunately, the right-wing media have had great success in portraying unions in negative terms, as enemies of the economy and power-mad self-serving extremists. Demonizing trade unions in this way has had the effect of discouraging many people from joining a union, but the trade union struggle to create fairer and more humane workplaces continues. Significantly, it parallels the social work commitment to creating a fairer and more humane society more broadly, despite neoliberal forces that are taking us alarmingly fast in the opposite direction.

Changes in management thinking

Alongside neoliberalism, we have to consider significant changes in management thinking. These changes are a profound effect on management practices in modern workplaces, and they are not coincidental: they reflect the wider sociopolitical context. They need to be seen as part of a wider movement that involves reducing worker power and increasing the power of managers and business owners.

One such change in management thinking that has had profound effects is what is known as business process re-engineering. This refers to the process of trying to make workplaces as efficient and economical as possible. While this may well be a wise and sensible process to enter into, unfortunately it has some very detrimental consequences. This is because the human resource implications of such processes were not thought through sufficiently well. For example, reducing staffing levels to the bare minimum required makes no allowance for sickness absence or other such events that mean that one or more workers is unavailable at any particular time – for example, in the gap between one member of staff leaving and a replacement being appointed and taking up the post following the completion of the notice period in their previous place of employment.

While maximizing efficiency and reducing costs as far as possible is to be welcomed in environmental terms due to the reduction in waste, there are other less positive implications to consider.

One such implication has been the development of flatter organizations – that is, organizations with fewer layers of management. While it makes sense to remove unnecessary layers of management, one of the consequences of this approach has been too many circumstances in which staff are left without adequate management support and oversight, and the managers will often find themselves in situations where there is a danger that they will be overwhelmed by the pressure of work they face – and this, of course, has negative implications for the staff they supervise. This also means that there are fewer options for advancement for basic grade staff, and this has implications in terms of career development (we shall return to this point in Chapter 8).

A second implication has been the development of what is commonly known as a 'more for less' mentality – the expectation that, through increased efficiency, better results can be achieved through the use of fewer resources. This has produced in many workplaces unrealistic targets, unreasonable levels of pressure on staff to achieve outcomes that previously required much higher levels of resources, including human resources. Again, an emphasis on reducing waste and unnecessary costs makes sense, but it is not a wise move if the adverse consequences of doing so act as a significant counterbalance to the benefits of the business process re-engineering approach. A common problem in many organizations is that the concept of 'human resources' becomes reduced to simply resources – the human element is neglected or omitted altogether (Bolton and Houlihan, 2007, Thompson, 2013a), hence the current emphasis on workplace well-being as a reaction against this (Kinder *et al.*, 2008). This runs counter to the employee empowerment approach that has begun to gain further attention in some places (Huq, 2015), with its highly significant recognition that empowered workers are more productive workers who are less likely to leave or cause problems for the organization (or its stakeholders). It also undermines the advances that have been made in terms of promoting the importance of dignity at work – for example in attempts to challenge and eradicate bullying and harassment.

It is therefore fair to say that the adoption of a business process re-engineering approach to management thinking has proven to be highly counterproductive and extremely problematic. It no longer holds the dominance it once did, but its influence is still clearly alive and well across many workplaces.

Another change in management thinking has been a greater emphasis on the need to develop leadership, recognizing that the pressures of the modern workplace in neoliberal times demand a much greater level of effective support and guidance. Linked to this has been a growing recognition of the need to address mental health and well-being issues in the workplace (Hasson and Butler, 2020). Again, this is part of the workplace well-being movement that has developed in response to the effects, among other things, of the disastrous implementation of an overzealous business process re-engineering approach and a general push in the direction of shifting power away from ordinary people to a privileged elite.

All this has significant implications for social work. As Thompson (2020) indicates, by its very nature, social work places practitioners in a situation best described as being 'caught in the middle' – that is, in the uncomfortable position between addressing the needs of the most vulnerable and disadvantaged members of our community and serving the wider interests of society at large. The very nature of social work is therefore a pressurized one. The additional pressures brought about by the factors outlined in this chapter have the potential to add up to an excessive level of pressure that leads to harmful stress. It is no coincidence that the question of stress in social work has been one that has been receiving significant attention for some time now. This is also why, in this book, the topic of stress receives considerable attention, such is the dangerous potential impact of excessive pressure on individuals, groups or whole organizations.

A further implication of this for social work is that we currently face what could be called 'a double whammy', in the sense that increasing inequality and the predominant governmental approach to such matters (in the form of austerity policies) reduces the resources available to social work personnel, while increasing the demand through the impact of greater social problems and fewer resources for addressing those problems. That is, austerity has had the effect of increasing poverty, mental health problems, abuse in various forms, alcohol- and drugs-related problems and, sadly, much more. Mendoza (2015, p. 7) highlights that austerity is driven by political ideology, an ideology that suits the socioeconomic interests of capital better than those of labour: 'Austerity is not a short-term disruption to balance the books. It is the demolition of the welfare state – transferring the UK from social democracy to corporate power'.

Consequently, what we have seen is an increasing gap between what is being asked of social workers and the resources available to address those demands as part of a process of moving from a welfare state to a residual one. This calls for a high level of effective leadership, but, as we shall see, the results in terms of promoting more and better leadership have been mixed.

Stress and surviving

How the term stress is used in everyday conversation and in a technical and legal sense are very different. It is important to recognize this, as confusing the two usages can be very misleading (Thompson, 2019a). This is not to say that it is in any sense 'wrong' to use the term stress in a loose, colloquial sense, but we do need to be aware of the differences between such usage and the formal understanding of stress.

In everyday conversation, pressure and stress tend to be used interchangeably. However, from a technical and legal point of view, the two need to be understood as different (albeit linked). This is because the Health and Safety Executive (and thus the legal system) conceive of stress as the point when levels of pressure exceed our ability to cope with them. That is, stress is understood as not just pressure in a general sense, but specifically pressure that is overwhelming the individual's ability to cope with it – that is, pressure that is doing harm.

Such harm can be to health, well-being, relationships, quality and quantity of work and various other aspects of our lives. Consequently, when people say that 'stress is good for you', they are not using stress in its legal sense. It is pressure, provided it is within manageable parameters, that is – or can be – good for you. This is one of the reasons why it is important to be clear about the distinction between pressure and stress: a manager telling a frazzled employee that 'stress is good for you' could be the last straw. It shows a lack of understanding of managers' health and safety responsibility towards employees

It can be helpful to think of pressure as neutral, in the sense that it can be positive or negative, while stress is always negative. Pressure is positive when it is motivating, rewarding, stimulating and even thrilling. However, if there is too much pressure, too many pressures or too long without a break from pressure, the result is negative. And that is where stress enters the picture, where the pressures are so great that they do us harm in one or more of the ways outlined above.

We can therefore understand 'surviving in social work' as meaning a combination of: (i) keeping pressures within manageable limits in whatever reasonable ways we can; and (ii) returning to a manageable level of pressure as soon as practicably possible if or when the line has been crossed into harmful stress.

Consistent with the overall message of this book, we also need to be aware that it is vitally important to recognize that 'surviving' does not have to be a solo project. The common tendency for stress to be individualized (thereby serving to pathologize the individual by presenting them as weak or inadequate) needs to be challenged and replaced with an approach rooted in solidarity, mutual support and a recognition that stress can happen to anyone, not just to people who 'can't cut it' or who need to 'get out of the kitchen' if they can't stand the heat. A macho approach to stress is highly problematic (for a fuller discussion of these issues, see Thompson, 2019a).

Stress and thriving

If we are to not only survive, but actually thrive, then we need to make sure that we are keeping our pressures within manageable limits, while also supporting others in doing so. The more mutual support there is, the greater the foundations for best practice will be.

By supporting one another, we help to break down the harmful idea that stress is the sign of a weak individual. We need to see it as a sign that there is something wrong that needs attention, but not necessarily wrong in the individual – we need to look at it more holistically (hence the emphasis on the macro as well as the micro in Chapter 3 and on what we can learn from the research in Chapter 4).

It can also be helpful to think about stress as it relates to the citizens that we serve. Traditionally, the focus has been on *occupational* stress, as if problems from excessive pressures arise only in the workplace. There is much to be gained in terms of direct practice to consider explicitly to what extent stress is playing a part in the lives of clients with a view to potentially identifying ways of reducing pressures until they reach a manageable – and, ideally, comfortable – level.

In terms of both our own pressures and those of other people, we support, we should also be aware that there is a positive side to pressure when it is not allowed to reach harmful levels. We mention this because we are aware that people who have found themselves in stressful situations will often avoid pressure as much as possible thereafter – a sort of once-bitten-twice-shy sort of approach. This can then prove to be very self-limiting – self-disempowering in fact. It acts as an obstacle to the motivation and satisfaction to be gained from a *reasonable* level of pressure.

After someone has been through a very stressful period, whether or not that involves sickness absence, it is understandable that it can take a while to get strength and confidence back on track. However, there is also a danger that people can get stuck in a low-pressure approach to life that they find frustrating and dispiriting (and, ironically, the pressures of this can lead to stress). What is needed, then, is a balanced approach to pressure – not too much, not too little. That will then serve as a firm basis for working towards thriving.

Conclusion

As if social work were not demanding enough in its own right, what we have outlined in this chapter is that there have been significant changes over time in the wider sociopolitical sphere that have had far-reaching consequences for the workplace. Realistically, what we have to recognize is that there cannot be any magic answers. However, being aware of the context helps us to have a fuller picture, so that we can better understand what we are dealing with.

It also gives us a framework for addressing the issues, both individually and collectively, and that will be a major theme of the chapters that follow. Perhaps most importantly of all, understanding this wider context can help us to de-pathologize the experiences that many people in social work are having – that is, to move away from the idea that anyone who is struggling to cope with the current level of pressure is somehow weak or inadequate. We all have limits to how much pressure we can cope with, and in modern circumstances, it is not at all surprising that significant numbers of people are finding it very difficult to manage the levels of pressure they face. In our view, this is an indication that there are problems in the wider context of the workplace in general and the social work context in particular that need addressing. It is not a sign of weakness in an individual, but rather a reflection of the enormity of the challenges we all face in these circumstances that are so far from being social work friendly.

It is our hope that you will appreciate that we do not have simple formula answers to present to you, but what we do offer should help to put you in a much stronger position in terms of understanding the complexities of the challenges we face, to feel empowered on a personal level to address them more effectively and, perhaps most importantly of all, fully appreciate the importance of pulling together and supporting one another through these difficult times in a spirit of solidarity.

Chapter 2: Social Work in Context

Introduction

In this chapter, we review the current state of social work in the context of major changes in working life over the years that have added significant pressures to a vocation that is already, by its very nature, a highly challenging enterprise. In Chapter 1 we commented briefly on the impact of this wider context on social work. Here we look at that impact – and its implications – in more detail. In particular, we shall be focusing on eight sets of issues, each one of which plays an important role in shaping the current circumstances that social workers face.

By exploring this range of topics, we are aiming to paint a fuller picture of how and why social work is so pressurized. This should help us to have a better grasp of the challenges we face so that we are better placed to tackle them, while also laying a foundation that can be built on in the discussions that appear in the chapters that follow.

We begin by clarifying some of the main reasons why social work is such a challenging occupational choice (albeit consistently a popular occupational choice).

The challenging nature of social work

For the first of the eight, we return to the point we touched on in Chapter 1, namely that social work is highly challenging by its very nature. If people were not facing difficulties, it is highly unlikely that we would be in their lives. Social work is therefore intrinsically bound up with problems and challenges – we necessarily operate in a context of problems, unmet needs, distress, suffering and pain. This fact is, of course, also a major facet of what makes social work so rewarding and stimulating, in so far as the richness of experience a career in social work offers can enhance the quality of our lives in ways that few other professions can (Collins, 2019).

This is partly due to our status as caring professionals who are 'caught in the middle'. However, that is not the whole story; there are other important issues to consider, including the tensions between caring and control. It has long been established that social work operates at the intersection of the personal and the social, and one of the implications of this is that our focus on caring also includes an element of control at times. For example, in trying to be caring by protecting children from abuse, we are often involved in mechanisms of control in relation to the perpetrator (or others who may be shielding the perpetrator).

Many people feel uncomfortable with this aspect of our work, but the reality is that it will often be necessary to engage in elements of control in order to be effective in caring. The key point is that social work necessarily involves the exercise of power, and so it is essential that we use such power ethically and responsibly. This involves making sure that any control elements are in the service of caring and not for purposes of control in their own right. For example, certain individuals with severe learning disabilities may have to have restrictions placed on their behaviour if it presents a danger to themselves or others. Where such power is being exercised, it needs to be done ethically, responsibly and, of course, proportionately.

Of course, a major part of this is ensuring that our use of power is not discriminatory in any way, hence the emphasis in social work education on recognizing and challenging discrimination and oppression.

Feeling unduly uncomfortable with the exercising of power can be highly problematic, as it may prevent us from tuning in to the implications of using such power (people who use power without realizing they are doing so can be highly dangerous). At the other extreme, people who are too comfortable with exercising power can also be practising dangerously by being complacent. A balanced approach is therefore called for.

These are very complex issues that we do not intend to explore in more detail here. But, we do want to acknowledge that having to operate within this difficult tension between caring and control can bring a certain amount of pressure, especially when those people we deal with, whether members of the general public or other professionals, are not aware of the significance of these issues or appreciate the complexities involved.

Social work is also characterized by a range of other ethical dilemmas – for example, in terms of operating in 'the best interests' of various members or sectors of the community, which at times can bring us into conflict with the people we are trying to serve, support, protect and empower. For example in the mental health field, we may be required at times to encourage people to do what they do not feel comfortable with – for example, someone struggling with depression being supported to change aspects of not only their behaviour, but also their emotional response to situations. To avoid ethical problems and the dangers of acting in a discriminatory or repressive way, it is essential that social workers are tuned in to the complexities involved in these issues and are prepared to think carefully about them. This, of course, is another potential source of pressure for social workers to contend with.

But even that is not the whole story. There is also the emotional intensity of the work to bear in mind. We will often be dealing with people who are distressed, grieving, traumatized, disturbed in one or more ways and struggling to deal with the emotional challenges that they currently face. We have to be very careful how we handle such situations to ensure that we do not become overloaded with the emotional strains involved in the situation. That is quite a skilful and demanding role, hence the strong emphasis these days on the significance of emotional intelligence and emotional resilience (Howe, 2008; Thompson, 2013b).

Being emotionally overloaded can lead to burnout and harmful emotional distance (potentially harmful to all concerned, a point to which we shall return below). Likewise, emotional overinvolvement can lead to some highly complex entanglements and potentially inappropriate practice (in terms of professional boundaries), as well as emotional strain. What is needed, then, is a balanced approach to how we react to the emotional dimension of social work.

Media misrepresentation

There are issues relating to media scapegoating that are also part of the contemporary social work scene. For example, the work of Ray Jones (2014) on the case of Baby Peter, where the work of social workers was strongly misrepresented in dangerous ways, has highlighted the harm that unscrupulous media professionals can cause. Baby Peter (Connelly) died as a result of abuse and, although it emerged that there had been mistakes made in efforts to protect him from harm, the Sun newspaper launched a vitriolic attack on the social work personnel involved that amounted to a campaign of vilification – a reaction that went far beyond what was justified by the circumstances of the case. It was, of course, also the Sun newspaper that was heavily criticized for its misrepresentation of the Hillsborough tragedy – see Scraton (2016) – and so this reaction to the Baby Peter case was not a new development in their approach to journalism.

Indeed, it has to be recognized that, in some respects, social work is no exception in terms of biased and inaccurate reporting. There is a discernible general blaming approach on the part of the media to professions in general, with few exceptions, in so far as good news does not sell newspapers or draw attention to media companies and the messages they are trying to put out. Bad news and criticism of professionals is the norm for most people in most circumstances. Consider, for example, how stories about crime will often be critical of the police, whether or not such criticisms are justified (and whether or not anyone has taken the trouble to try and find out whether or not they are justified). Stories about how people have (allegedly) fallen short in terms of their professional duties have more appeal than stories about people doing their jobs conscientiously and effectively.

However, because social work is involved in what Thompson (2020a) calls 'doing society's dirty work', social workers are often an easy target for such unethical journalistic practices. By 'doing society's dirty work' what Thompson means is dealing with many of the problems that most people in society would prefer not to think about. They would be happier if we could sweep these under the carpet and pretend that they do not exist.

The role of the media is therefore potentially quite problematic, and yet another source of pressure for social workers.

Infinite demand and finite supply

We also need to take account of the perennial issue of social work having a finite supply of resources (including personal resources) matched against the potential for infinite demand. That is, while there is potentially no end to what social workers can be asked to do at any given time, there is a limitation on what can be done in response. For example, limits generally have to be set in terms of how extensive a care package can be for older or disabled people due to budgetary limitations (demand may be limitless, but resources are certainly not, especially in an era characterized by the impact of austerity). There can, however, be significant gaps between what can be made available and the optimal level. There can also be significant differences between what, say, family members feel should be available and what is formally assessed as what is necessary. Similarly, there is also the potential to invest more and more in preventative work.

Consequently, a significant skill set in social work is the ability to prioritize and manage workload pressures effectively (although traditionally this has not been a major feature of social work education, sadly). What has intensified the problem in recent years has been the underfunding of services due to the political policy of austerity as part of the wider picture of a diminishing commitment to public services as part of neoliberalism (Mendoza, 2015), as discussed in Chapter 1.

Tension between infinite demand and finite supply is one of the things that can make social work a highly pressurized place to operate, but, as we shall see in later chapters, there are ways and means of managing this tension effectively, if we are sufficiently tuned in to the issues involved.

What can add to the pressures is that people who do not appreciate the significance of limited supply can become hostile when they mistakenly assume that they are being denied something to which they are entitled. This will generally be the individuals concerned and/or their family members, but it can also be neighbours and even, in some circumstances, fellow professionals. This highlights the importance of 'setting out our stall', as we shall discuss later – that is, making it clear what we can and cannot do (Thompson, 2018a). Being effective in doing so does not guarantee that we will not encounter any unpleasant adverse responses, but it does reduce the likelihood considerably if we are clear about what we can and cannot do, what can and cannot be offered (that is, the boundaries of our role).

Leadership difficulties

There are also concerns about leadership and the perceived lack of a sufficiently high quality of leadership and people management. Historically, this can partly be traced to a traditional lack of emphasis in the social work world on leadership and management skills, combined with a lack of emphasis in the wider management education field on leadership in public services. The major emphasis of most leadership texts courses and other learning resources is primarily on the business world, as if to suggest that leadership is not required in public services. We are thankfully beginning to see the process of rectifying this situation, with more and more emphasis now being placed on the need to develop effective leadership in public services in general and social work in particular (Gilbert, 2005; Gilbert and Thompson, 2019).

What makes this need all the more pressing, of course, is the huge pressures that social work managers face in trying to support overstretched practitioners in highly demanding circumstances, while also having to manage the demands that come to them from above in terms of a managerialist approach (one rooted in neoliberal thinking that is not conducive to effective management and human resources practices). By managerialist what we mean is rooted in the neoliberal assumption that public services work best when they are treated in the same way as businesses, with profit targets replaced by performance targets. Such an approach has been heavily criticized for trying to fit square pegs into round holes, not recognizing the complex differences business process, culture, values and aims and those of public services (Thompson, 2016b).

The predominance of managerialist expectations in the neoliberal era has put undue pressure on managers who are being asked to manage a public service while looking through business lenses. This combines with the pressures added by business process re-engineering, as discussed in Chapter 1 (the more-for-less mentality) to produce a very uncomfortable working environment for social work managers. It is no wonder, then, that, without adequate training and support, so many managers find it difficult to offer the quality and extent of leadership and management that people need. We are beginning to see important changes in this regard, but it is fair to say that we still have a long way to go yet in addressing the very real problems in the field in which elements of the system set so many managers up, if not to fail, then at least to have a major struggle on their hands.

One important aspect of this problem can be identified as difficulties in the transferability of skills. In some ways, it could be argued that currently practising social workers are well placed to become the managers and leaders of the future, given the development of so many relevant skills, such as effective communication, thinking holistically, problem solving, conflict management, empowerment and so on. However, the assumption that these skills will be readily transferable by most practitioners who become managers is not always borne out in practice. We have come across many examples of people who have been highly competent social workers, drawing on a wide range of appropriate skills that are just as relevant in management as they are in direct social work practice, but who have, for whatever reason, struggled to put those skills into practice in the new context.

Part of this, no doubt, is the unwarranted assumption that any set of skills can be readily transferred from one context to another without any focus on facilitating the process of doing so. One of the consequences of this is that it can often be assumed that the problems that so many people face in social work organizations these days are down to a lack of competence in managers. This is both unfair and inaccurate. In our experience, the majority of managers are trying to do their best in difficult circumstances, but many will be struggling to adapt their skills to a new context without proper training, mentorship and/or other forms of support.

We have already commented on the 'caught in the middle' tension in social work, but there is another dimension to this. This is because managers can also be caught in the middle between the social work values that have featured in their days as a practitioner and the values of managerialism as part of neoliberalism that they find themselves under pressure to adopt. Managerialism is an approach to the workplace that has grown up as part of neoliberal thinking. It involves focusing on targets and performance indicators to try and make public service management as much like business management as possible, reflecting the lack of commitment to public services (and the lack of understanding of the crucial differences between public services and business practices). It therefore needs to be understood that what we are talking about in terms of leadership problems is not simply a lack of competence; the situation is far more complex than that, involving a range of factors, such as the ones touched on here.

These problems are of considerable significance, as effective leadership can make such a positive difference to the quality of working life, while poor or non-existent leadership can do immense harm. Part of this is that leadership affects how we make sense of our working lives, of what our work means to us. As Grint (2005) explains:

> Great leadership has the potential to excite people to extraordinary levels of achievement. But it is not only about performance; it is also about meaning ... Leaders at all levels make a difference to performance. They do so because they make performance meaningful.
>
> (p. 2)

As we shall note later, meaning is a core element of spirituality and workplace well-being is very much a spiritual matter. We shall therefore return to this point later.

A major focus of leadership is the ability to shape the organizational culture (as a framework of meaning) in a positive direction (Thompson, 2016a). Organizational cultures are very powerful influences on people's thoughts, feelings and actions. They become the unquestioned norm, the day-to-day reality of what happens in practice, and this is what gives organizational culture its power. Leaders therefore need to have the skills and awareness to be able to understand how organizational cultures operate in general and their own in particular and to be in a position to influence it in a positive direction. This is part of a steep learning curve that so many social work managers are on in this day and age, following a long period of time when leadership and management skills were taken for granted, as if it could be assumed that a good social worker would automatically become a good manager in due course. This theme of leadership as a process of culture shaping will feature in our discussions in later chapters, as it is an important aspect of the situation that we currently face in terms of surviving and thriving.

Another aspect of leadership that is significant is that cultures involving an excess of pressure can easily serve as a basis for a harmful set of vicious circles. For example, excessive pressure can lead to low morale; this tends to lead to a defeatist, negative approach that can easily become destructive cynicism. That defeatism in turn can reinforce low morale. What is significant about this – in fact, highly significant, as we shall note in later chapters – is that low morale has the effect of, in effect, doubling the workload. What we mean by this is that people working in a context of a low-morale culture will probably only achieve something in the region of half of the productivity that they could have achieved if morale were at a much higher level.

Low morale is problematic in many ways (blocking learning, stifling creativity and so on), and therefore an issue to be taken seriously. What is particularly dangerous is when it is 'normalized' – that is, a point is reached where people expect morale to be low as a matter of course. A significant consequence of this is that little or no effort is made to address the causes of such low morale. The defeatism that is so characteristic of low morale thereby serves to lock people into such a negative culture. This then becomes a major challenge of leadership, especially for leaders who themselves are struggling to cope with their own negativity.

One final point around leadership that we want to emphasize is the significant role of self-leadership – that is, the ability to shape the mindset and approach that we adopt in relation to the challenges we face. What this means in practice is being able to resist the temptation to participate in a culture of negativity, defeatism and cynicism and, instead, to adopt an attitude of trying to do the best we can in difficult circumstances, rather than making difficult circumstances worse by becoming defeatist and cynical. One implication of this is that people who are employed as leaders need first to succeed in self-leadership if they are to be effective in leading others. We shall return to this point in Chapter 3.

Consumerism

Next, we need to consider the significance of consumerism in contemporary social work. What we mean by consumerism is the way in which developments in social work over many years now have led to an undue focus on service provision. The traditional focus of social work has been on problem solving and empowerment – that is, using our knowledge, skills and values to work towards empowering people to solve their own problems where possible, and to support them as fully as we reasonably can in addressing the problems they face. Consequently, a key part of traditional social work practice has been an emphasis not on providing or commissioning services, but on engaging in empowering forms of practice to avoid the need for services where possible.

The emphasis on outcome-focused practice can be understood as, in large part, a counterbalance to this consumerist approach. For example, one of the present authors (Neil) has been involved in running many training courses around outcome-focused practice where participants have made comments to the effect of: 'I hadn't thought about it before, but I realize now that I have been driving to people's houses thinking about what services I could offer them, rather than how I could help them address their problems and their needs'. While such honesty came across as refreshing, the prevalence of such thinking was deeply concerning.

A consumerist approach, with its emphasis on rationing scarce resources, has become so well established that we now have a significant generation gap. Both authors, for example, have had conversations with many young social workers who, throughout their career have only ever known a care management process of rationing scarce resources, and therefore have little or no experience of undertaking empowering forms of social work that involve making use of a wide range of social work methods and tools (de Mönnink, 2017; Thompson and Stepney, 2018; Thompson, 2020b).

In some ways, consumerism can be seen to be self-defeating, in so far as an emphasis on service provision (rather than problem-solving efforts to avoid the need for the services where possible) has placed immense pressures on limited budgets, often leading to the resource 'pie' being divided up into smaller and smaller portions, often portions that are not enough to meet people's needs because service resources are being stretched too thinly. An approach based on empowerment and problem solving, by contrast, protects limited budgets by preserving service provision only for those people where there are no other ways of addressing their needs.

Examples of such approaches would include:

- An elderly woman struggling to cope on her own receives no help from her extended family due to an ongoing conflict and is therefore assessed as needing an extensive care package. However, a social worker making good use of mediation skills helps to resolve the family conflict and thereby avoids the need for a care package.

- A disabled man is on a waiting list for a place at a day centre. He lacks the confidence to make use of local community services. However, a social worker arranges for a volunteer to befriend him and take him on a tour of local community facilities.

- A young mother with learning disabilities relies heavily on the support of a family aide until a social worker arranges for her to attend a parenting group. The learning (and social support) she gains from this group enables her to reduce her reliance on a family aide.

Why the interest in doing social work?

One further set of issues we need to consider in terms of the current social work context is the fundamental question of why we do it – why do so many people want to develop their careers in such difficult, demanding, challenging work roles that often result in little or no appreciation and often unfair criticism?

A key part of the response to this question must surely be our values, particularly our commitment to compassion. One of the very worrying aspects of the contemporary social work scene is that it can become very difficult to hold onto our values and to remain fully compassionate when we face such undue pressures, often in circumstances where there is insufficient support for us and any efforts that we are making to do our best in difficult circumstances. However, as we shall see, holding onto our values and sustaining our commitment to compassion are fundamental aspects of not only surviving, but also thriving (Moss and Thompson, 2020).

Similarly, a key part of this is our commitment to social justice. A major feature of the motivation for at least the majority of people entering social work is to make a contribution to a fairer and more humane society. Inevitably, therefore, social justice needs to feature in this. This in itself is a two-edged sword, in the sense that: (i) trying to promote social justice in the present sociopolitical climate and in the resource-starved contemporary scene is an exceedingly difficult task; and (ii) our commitment to social justice can be a fundamental part of what keeps us going, what plays a major role in making sure that we are able to keep our head above water and to continue, despite the obstacles, to press for a fairer and more humane society.

Values are therefore an important aspect of surviving and thriving. As Kouzes and Posner (2007) comment:

> Values are empowering. We are much more in control of our own lives ... when we're clear about our personal values. When values are clear we don't have to rely on direction from someone in authority. ... Values also motivate. They keep us focused on why we're doing what we're doing and on the ends toward which we're striving. Values are the banners that fly as we persist, as we struggle, as we toil. We refer to them when we need to replenish our energy.
>
> (p. 53)

This is not the only time we shall be emphasizing the importance of values.

Another factor to acknowledge is the importance of self-respect. Despite the prevalence of unfair media coverage, we have to recognize that social work is a very positive force in contemporary society. Social workers play an exceptionally important role. The gap between the reality of the social worth of what we do and how it is often perceived by others is of major proportions. However, we should not allow this to distract us from the fact that what we do has considerable value and, for the most part, we do it exceptionally well in very trying circumstances (with occasional mistakes, as will happen in any profession or vocational group from time to time). We need constantly to reaffirm that we are playing a vitally important role in making our society as fair, humane and compassionate as it can possibly be in such difficult circumstances. Maintaining our self-respect, despite not having it reinforced in the same way that, for example, nurses have theirs reinforced, should not prevent us from taking pride in what we do. We say this in full awareness that the lack of external validation and affirmation makes this much more difficult, but it does not make it impossible. This is another reason why we need to focus on solidarity, as validating and affirming one another has an important role to play in helping people survive and plays no small part in helping us thrive.

Ideally, what we do should be fully appreciated and celebrated by wider society. But, given the fact that we are 'doing society's dirty work', that ideal is highly unlikely to be realized without a major change in society's attitude towards people who are in some ways struggling with the demands placed on them or, to use Bob Dylan's turn of phrase, 'bent out of shape by society's pliers'.

Our self-respect should enable us to recognize, benefit from and even celebrate the satisfactions of making a positive difference to so many people in so many ways – and still manage to do this so well, despite so many discouragements brought about by the nature of the work we do and society's attitudes towards so many of the problems that we are involved in addressing in our day-to-day work.

Balancing positives and negatives

In an important text on 'positive social work', Collins (2019) urges us not to lose sight of the positives of social work, even in today's exceptionally challenging times:

> What is it that 'keeps us going' in social work? What is it that sustains us? What helps us to maintain positive approaches to, and obtain satisfaction from, our work? The vast majority of colleagues who I have worked with have remained in social work, or social work education, despite stress, demands, limited resources, and high workloads. I considered what factors had helped me to enjoy a career of 50 years in social work and social work education. These included the ever-present, ever-expanding variety of challenges, a belief that one had things to offer in helping others, enthusiasm, and a 'desire to make a difference', which provoked an ongoing commitment to social work. However, at the present time, the political and organisational context for social work ... is enormously challenging. Whilst recognising this, it seems very important to consider the ways in which we can both establish and maintain positive approaches as social workers, along with the knowledge, understanding, and skills that can help us with the task.
>
> (p. vi)

This takes us back to the concept of realism, by which we mean not adopting a rose-tinted optimism that fails to recognize the major difficulties we currently face, nor a defeatist pessimism that sees only the negatives and disregards the positives. If we are to survive, we need to be aware of the negatives and the dangers they present, but we also need to be tuned in to the positives that counterbalance them to some considerable degree. And, if we are to go beyond surviving and achieve actual thriving, we need to capitalize fully on those positives – especially solidarity – and not allow them to be submerged in a culture of low morale.

If we focus only on the negatives and lose sight of the positives, we face a very real risk of burnout – a highly damaging and destructive condition.

Burnout

Burnout is a condition characterized by three main characteristics:

- *Exhaustion or energy depletion* This goes beyond 'normal' tiredness. It refers to circumstances where we reach the point that we are struggling to summon up enough energy to get through the day. Everything is a struggle.

- *Distancing* This refers to a strong tendency to withdraw ourselves, to become emotionally distant and aloof. It is, in effect, a form of disengagement as a defence mechanism.

- *Ineffectiveness* People who are burnt out struggle to be effective in their work (and in aspects of their home life). Normal levels of competence are reduced, sometimes to dangerous levels.

In social work we often come across people whose attempted solutions become a problem in their own right (for example, someone who develops a drink problem in an attempt to escape other problems in their life). Burnout is very similar to this, in the sense that, while it is clearly a problem itself, it arises as an attempted solution – a way of dealing with excessive pressures. It is as if we are trying to develop a protective layer that separates us from the emotional and other demands of our work.

This is the irony of burnout – it is an attempted solution, but it turns out to be highly problematic and actually leaves us less well equipped to deal with the pressures we face. It therefore contributes to yet more vicious circles. The more burnt out we are, the harder it is to cope with our pressures, and the more pressures we face, the more burnt out we become.

Burnout is likely to be problematic for all involved in the situation, not just the individual(s) concerned. Managers, colleagues, clients, carers and others can all lose out as a result of having to work with someone who is burnt out, someone who is emotionally detached, whose heart is not in the job and who is functioning at a level far below the optimum (and quite possibly far below the acceptable).
It is therefore essential that we do what we reasonably can – individually and collectively – to prevent burnout in the first place and to support one another whenever it does arise. How effective we are at addressing the problem of burnout will therefore play a key part in our efforts to survive. Allowing burnout to feature in our workplaces (as some cultures sadly do), will hamper efforts to survive and will act as a major, quite possibly insurmountable, obstacle to thriving.

Unfortunately, where people are operating in circumstances where they are overloaded, they can withdraw into the sort of 'security bubble' we discussed in Chapter 1, and this can lead to their not noticing that one or more colleagues is burning out. Indeed, retreating into such a bubble may actually be a step in the direction of burnout in its own right.

Conclusion

We have covered a lot of ground in one relatively short chapter, and so there is much to consider further. However, a key element of this boils down to what sort of life we want. Are we looking for a quiet life that steadily ticks away, without making any positive difference? Or, are we seeking a challenging life that makes a positive difference in difficult and challenging times?

The latter clearly makes life more meaningful and satisfying if we are able to manage the challenges involved, which is basically what this book is about. We fully recognize the significance and extent of these challenges, what we want to do here is to look at the other side of the coin in terms of the steps that we can take – individually and collectively – to continue to make social work a positive aspect of society, while also making sure that our own mental health and well-being are safeguarded.

These are spiritual challenges, in the sense that, regardless of whether or not we are religious, we all have spiritual needs and spiritual challenges (Moss and Thompson, 2019). We all face the challenge of making our lives meaningful, having a sense of purpose and direction and of being part of something bigger than ourselves. This is a theme that we shall be visiting later, as we want to emphasize that the issues we are addressing are not simply about tricks of the trade or tips and techniques for managing pressure in difficult circumstances. Important though these are, we are trying to present a broader picture than that, one that recognizes the need for a holistic understanding and strategic approach to how to make sure that we not only survive, but also manage to thrive – that is, to achieve the best results we can while remaining safe in terms of our own needs and our own well-being.

To return to the work of Collins (2019):

> However, are social workers trapped? Practitioners can turn to alternative concepts, to alternative models. There are positive ideas which continue to motivate social workers to help them to survive, to sustain themselves, to take up challenges, to thrive and flourish. There are positive discourses, options and choices beyond narratives focused upon role ambiguity, role conflict, demands, pressure, stress, exhaustion, and burnout. Yes, pressure, stress, and burnout are clearly evident, but social workers also experience considerable rewards and job satisfaction alongside the difficulties. In conjunction with their teams, colleagues, managers, and organisations social workers can tolerate, can resist negativity, working both individually and together to recognise, to work with, and towards alternatives.
>
> (p. 1)

In other words, we can make the choice to pull together to do the best we can in difficult circumstances, rather than make the situation worse by allowing negativity, defeatism and cynicism to become the norm. That is the immense challenge we face. But, of course, we do not have to face it alone and unsupported. The more we are able to succeed in supporting one another in moving forward positively together, the stronger a position we will be in and the more effective we can be in not only surviving, but also thriving. As we make our way through the remaining chapters, we will see that this is an important recurring theme that merits our close attention, as it has the potential to be extremely useful.

Chapter 3: Macro Meets Micro

Introduction

The idea of taking account of both individual (psychological) and wider contextual (sociological) factors is well established in the longstanding *psychosocial* basis of social work. We need to apply the same logic to our own situation, as well as to the circumstances of the people we serve. That is, we need to incorporate an understanding of both psychological and sociological issues and how they relate to one another. People who look narrowly at the psychological dimension run the risk of failing to recognize the important role of power relations, cultural influences and structural constraints, thereby potentially reinforcing discrimination and oppression.

Bunting (2004) captures the point well:

> But we are crippled by one of the strongest illusions of our age, namely that we seek 'biographic solutions to structural contradictions', as the German sociologist Ulrich Beck puts it. We look for personal, private solutions to our problems, rather than identifying with others and achieving reform.
>
> (p. xxv)

On the other hand, those who look broadly at the wider context but fail to take account of the psychological implications for each individual concerned run the risk of dehumanizing the very people they are trying to help, and thereby oppressing them. Clearly, then, what is needed is an approach that takes account of both the micro and the macro factors involved.

What this means is that surviving needs to be based on understanding and, where appropriate, challenging the bigger picture, including poor working conditions, lack of management support and so on, *and* our own personal reactions (avoiding vicious circles, negativity, cynicism and burnout, and so on). We need to be able to develop a holistic picture that incorporates these wider aspects as well as our own personal contributions, just as we are expected to do in adopting a psychosocial approach to social work practice.

We shall first focus our attention on a number of macro-level factors and consider their significance. This will be followed by a parallel consideration of some very relevant micro-level factors. Then, before drawing the chapter to a close, we shall comment on the importance of recognizing how the macro and micro interact in a dialectical way (that is, each affecting the other in one or more ways).

Macro

As social workers with a grounding in anti-discriminatory practice, we should be well aware of the significance of the wider sociopolitical context in shaping people's lives, experiences, problems and potential solutions. We need to bear that wider context in mind when we consider our current circumstances and the challenges we face in terms of surviving and thriving. We need to appreciate that, just like in direct social work practice, what is happening in our workplaces is due to a complex mix of personal, cultural and structural factors. The cultural and structural factors are what we are placing under the heading of the macro-level context, that bigger picture in which personal thoughts, feelings and actions operate.

Pressure limits

We have already mentioned the pathologizing tendency of dominant approaches to stress, as if it were simply a matter of one or more individuals who are in some way out of their depth due to some aspect of their own capabilities. An appreciation of the macro level could help us to realize that much will depend on the wider context. For example, if we were to take somebody who is under a reasonable level of pressure and is coping quite well, perhaps even thriving under that level of pressure, and all the demands that they face, there is likely to be little chance of stress arising. If this person were incredibly skilful in managing high levels of pressure, they might be able to continue to cope even if there was a doubling of their workload. But, what if their workload were to be doubled again? Of course, if pressures continue to grow, there will come a time when pressures exceed the ability to cope.

Sooner or later, everyone faces the reality that there will be a limit in terms of the pressure that we can cope with. We can therefore see that a simplistic idea that managing pressure is solely a matter for individuals and their own capability is far from adequate and is, in fact, quite dangerous. It fails to take account of the significance of an overloaded system. If the system itself is overloaded, then it is unfair and potentially oppressive to regard anyone who struggles within that system as incapable. In effect, adopting such a narrow view colludes with unrealistic expectations at the expense of the health and well-being of practitioners (and managers).

It is unsafe to assume that people can cope with an unlimited amount of pressure. Where a system is overloaded, then clearly the problem needs to be addressed at a systemic level (taking us back to our theme of leadership). While individuals and groups within the system can take steps to cope as effectively as possible, these actions can only offer short-term solutions while the wider problem of an overloaded system goes unheeded.

The role of support

Thompson (2019a) emphasizes the importance of support as a key determinant of whether or not people become stressed. The level, extent and value of support offered will be a major factor in determining whether or not a highly pressurized worker experiences stress. The quality and quantity of that support will, similarly, then depend on other wider organizational factors – for example, the extent, quality and value of support the managers receive from their own managers. There will also be further organizational factors arising from the nature of organizational culture.

Some cultures have a very macho approach to workload pressures, a sort of 'if you can't stand the heat, get out of the kitchen' approach, while others are much more sensitive and understanding and therefore supportive. It needs to be remembered that organizational cultures are very powerful. They operate in very subtle ways, generally unnoticed – indeed, it is this subtlety and invisible operation that give culture so much of its power. Cultures can be crucial in either making a situation much better or much worse – indeed, the culture can often be a make or break factor in terms of whether or not an individual manages to survive the intense pressures they face.

Cultures are multidimensional, and one key dimension is precisely that of support. In terms of how supportive they are, cultures can vary from extremely supportive (where people get a real boost from the ethos of the team and/or the wider organization) to extremely unsupportive (where there is bullying, for example, or other unhelpful behaviours and assumptions).

It can therefore be helpful to think about what the nature of your culture is in terms of where you currently work (or are studying) – which aspects help and which aspects hinder in terms of providing a safe and supportive environment in which to work?

Victim blaming

The discourse of victim blaming we mentioned earlier is a well-established phenomenon in many aspects of society (for example, poor people being blamed for their own poverty as a result of supposed 'fecklessness', without any consideration of the socioeconomic circumstances that are major factors in the development of such poverty). Illouz (2012) highlights the role sociology can play in helping us to develop a more holistic approach:

> Precisely because we live in a time where the idea of individual responsibility reigns supreme, the vocation of sociology remains vital. In the same way that at the end of the nineteenth century it was radical to claim that poverty was the result not of dubious morality or weak character, but of systematic economic exploitation, it is now urgent to claim not that the failures are the result of weak psyches, but rather the vagaries and miseries of our emotional life are shaped by institutional arrangements.

> (p. 4)

Sadly, what has grown up over the decades is a similar victim-blaming approach to anyone who is seen to be struggling with immense workload pressures. A moment ago we mentioned that workplace cultures can either help or hinder when it comes to support. One aspect of a hindrance would be a culture that reflects victim blaming by labelling anyone who seeks support as weak or inadequate (rather than wise and sensible). A culture that stigmatizes asking for support is a dangerous and destructive culture.

Victim blaming serves to mask the wider processes and vested interests that keep the wheels of society turning in ways that benefit the power elite. Presenting, for example, a structural problem such as underfunding as if it were a matter of personal inadequacy is a classic example of hegemony. This is a technical term that refers to how relations of dominance are maintained through ideology – that is, the power of ideas. Social institutions, such as the media and the education system, feed an ideology (a set of ideas rooted in power relations) that serves to justify existing power relations and the privileges they bestow (Thompson, 2018b). Failures in underfunded public services are widely presented not in systemic terms, but in terms of individual failings. Consider, for example, how failures in the NHS tend to be portrayed as examples of poor management, rather than reflections of underfunding. Again, we are not suggesting that poor management does not exist, but rather highlighting how macro-level problems tend to be reinterpreted as micro-level failings, as this leaves the relations of dominance intact.

As we shall see in Chapter 4, there is a growing research base that highlights the significance of poor working conditions and the contribution that these make to the struggle to survive in modern social work. It should be clear, then, that a narrow individualistic, psychological approach to these issues is woefully inadequate. At the very least, we need to have a good understanding of this wider picture so that we do not fall into the trap of making a bad situation worse by making already overstretched people feel guilty or inadequate because they are struggling to cope with unrealistic levels of pressure.

Unfortunately, one of the vicious circles that has developed in many places is for some overstretched managers to collude with the victim-blaming approach by using capability procedures as a stick with which to beat struggling practitioners. We say this because we have come across very many examples of practitioners who are understandably struggling with immense pressures, but who have been told by their managers that, if they do not do a better job, they will face capability procedures. This heavy-handed tactic is clearly counterproductive, as it simply serves to create additional pressures. It can easily become a self-fulfilling prophecy, in the sense that the extra pressure can lead to an even greater level of struggling on the part of the practitioner, which is then used to justify the capability procedures by painting a picture of someone who is 'not coping', rather than someone who, by virtue of circumstance, has been placed in a largely impossible situation.

This is not to say that capability procedures should never be used, but they should be limited to those circumstances where it is genuinely a matter of capability and not of unrealistic expectations.

Managerialism

We have already touched on the subject of managerialism, the neoliberal attempt to treat public services as if they are businesses. Its role in our current malaise means that it is worth exploring in more detail here.

Ballatt and Campling (2011) are rightly highly critical of managerialist approaches to the caring professions. Their comments are worth reproducing at length:

> There is evidence that, as well as supporting improvement, target- or indicator-driven activities can have, in themselves, a range of unhelpful unintended consequences. Researchers from the University of York and the University of St Andrews report a range of such consequences (Goddard *et al.*, 2000). They have found consistent evidence of:
> - *tunnel vision* – concentration on areas that are included in the performance indicator scheme, to the exclusion of other important areas
> - *suboptimisation* – the pursuit of narrow local objectives by managers, at the expense of the objectives of the organisation as a whole
> - *myopia* – concentration on short-term issues, to the exclusion of long-term criteria that may show up in performance measures only in many years' time
> - *measure fixation* – focusing on what is measured rather than the outcomes intended
> - *complacency* – a lack of motivation for improvement when comparative performance is deemed adequate
> - *ossification* – referring to the organisational paralysis that can arise from an excessively rigid system of measurement
> - *misrepresentation* – the deliberate manipulation of data, including

'creative' accounting and fraud, so that reported behaviour differs from actual behaviour.

- *gaming* – altering behaviour so as to obtain strategic advantage. Steve Illife covers similar ground, describing the risks of a system where economic factors outweigh professional imperatives in shaping GPs' behaviour. He describes three main risks: poor performance in domains where performance is not measured; hitting the target but missing the point; and discrepancies in data recording (Illife, 2008), p. 112). Even Chris Ham, health policy academic and head of the King's Fund, and a proponent of performance targets, acknowledges the dangers of disempowering front-line staff, stifling innovation and overloading the organisations providing care to patients (Ham, 2009). To this list we might add cynicism, disengagement and low morale in staff, and anxiety and mistrust in patients.

(p. 166)

Each of the ten concerns highlighted here merits closer attention:

- *Tunnel vision* – The narrow focus on targets and performance indicators in many areas has had the effect of excluding other important issues from the picture. Priorities can then become decided by arbitrary targets, rather than professional decision making, a dangerous situation in social work.

- *Suboptimization* – Similarly, the focus on specific local targets can easily lead to people losing sight of the overall aims of the organization. A holistic approach gives way to a much narrower focus. This can have implications in terms of ensuring that we are not losing sight of our wider social values.

- *Myopia* – Narrowing can also happen in terms of timescales, with short-term targets taking priority over longer-term goals. This can be highly problematic where longer-term plans are needed – for example, in circumstances where local authorities are acting as corporate parents.

- *Measure fixation* – 'What cannot be measured cannot be managed' is a longstanding management cliché that oversimplifies some complex issues. Of course, accurate management information is essential for planning, but it is only one consideration among many in terms of organizational success.

- *Complacency* – Focusing on hitting targets can encourage people to settle for good enough (surviving), rather than aim for the best results possible (thriving). If targets are the primary consideration, optimal outcomes tend to get squeezed out of the picture.

- *Ossification* – Adopting a pseudoscientific approach to management rooted in mathematics can easily generate a very rigid approach to working life. Such rigidity tends to stifle creativity and generate levels of anxiety that can lead to a form of organizational paralysis where no risks are taken.

- *Misrepresentation* – There are sadly many cases on record of people 'cooking the books' to make it look as though targets were met, when in reality they were not – for example, social workers registering on the computer that reviews have been done when they have not.

- *Gaming* – Leadership needs to be based on clarity, openness and honesty, but managerialism can take us in the opposite direction by encouraging people to play games in order to negotiate their way through the complex bureaucracy that stands in their way.

- *Cynicism, disengagement and low morale in staff* – We have already highlighted how much harm these matters can bring about. Managerialism, with all its flaws and little by way of benefits, has been a major contributor to such negativity by undermining professionalism.

- *Anxiety and mistrust in patients* – These various drawbacks, of course, do no favours to the people we serve. Understandably, they can experience a degree of alienation when faced with the various rigidities of managerialism and consequently feel anxious and mistrustful in response.

It should be clear, then, that managerialism, with its roots in neoliberal thinking, has created a number of problems for social work, and indeed for public services more broadly.

The irony here is that there is much that can be learned from the business world for public services. For example, the 'lean management' approach developed by the Toyota Motor Corporation has useful lessons for us around managing high levels of pressure as effectively as possible:

> We view errors as opportunities for learning. Rather than blaming individuals, the organization takes corrective actions and distributes knowledge about each experience broadly. Learning is a continuous company-wide process as superiors motivate and train subordinates; as predecessors do the same for successors; and as team members at all levels share knowledge with one another.
>
> (*The Toyota Way* document, 2001, cited in Liker, 2014, p. 250)

A key aspect of this philosophy is *hansei*, which links closely with the notion of reflective practice that we are very familiar with in social work. Literally, *hansei* means reflection, and it is often referred to as 'relentless reflection', meaning that is is not something that is done only on certain occasions. This fits well with the argument put forward by Thompson and Thompson (2018) that reflective practice needs to be understood as a core element of all good practice, and not something that is somehow set apart from it.

As Liker (2014) comments, quoting George Yamashina, who runs the Toyota Technical Center:

> In Japanese *hansei*, when you do something wrong, at first you must feel really, really sad. Then you must create a future plan to solve that problem and you must sincerely believe you will never make this type of mistake again. *Hansei* is a mindset, an attitude. *Hansei* and *kaizen* [continuous improvement] go hand in hand.
>
> (p. 257)

Contrast this with a blame culture with all its negative and debilitating effects.

What adds to the irony, though, is that Liker argues that these methods have often failed in reality because they have been implemented superficially. Emphasis has been placed on specific efficiency tools, rather than on making sure that the lean philosophy has been incorporated into the whole system of working and, importantly, the organizational culture.

What we want to emphasize here, therefore, is that there are alternatives to the currently rather dysfunctional managements systems, but any real and lasting changes must come from changes in the culture (which brings us back to leadership practices once again). Using ideas in a purely instrumental or technical way will not bring about the changes needed to improve the quality of working life.

The legal context

A key element of the macro-level picture is the legal context. When we are dealing with problematic levels of work pressure and consequent stress, we are in the domain of health and safety legislation. In a sense, this legislation mirrors our approach as adopted in this book. By this we mean that the health and safety legislation places a duty of care on both employers and employees. Employers have a duty of care towards their employees, which means that they are duty bound to take reasonable steps to keep their employees safe and free from harm.

This includes stress. Where employees are subject to health-affecting, harmful levels of pressure, this, in effect, becomes a health and safety matter. This is because it is basically illegal for employers to knowingly allow their employees to be operating in unduly hazardous situations (and stress is included in this) or to fail to take appropriate preventative measures to limit the chances of such harmful circumstances arising.

Health and safety duties, then, are not simply a matter of making sure that there are signs warning people of wet floors, that electrical appliances are properly earthed, and so on. It is much broader than this; it is about developing a health and safety culture in which proper and reasonable steps are taken to avoid harm to employees. What is meant by a 'health and safety culture' is a workplace where keeping people safe and healthy is woven into the very culture, rather than being an add on or even an afterthought (which is how it tends to be managed in many places). An organization that is allowing some or all of its employees to be harmed in some significant way by their level of work pressure is potentially in breach of health and safety legislation. But, simply complying with legislation is far from ideal. Making sure that health and safety issues are treated as bread and butter matters throughout the workplace is what we should be aiming for, including health and safety around stress.

The fact that this is an organizational culture issue takes us back to our theme of leadership and the importance of developing positive supportive cultures and moving away from harmful ones that simply make a bad situation worse.

Our approach to surviving in social work seeks to take full account of these legal obligations and to make the most of the protection that they offer. However, as we shall emphasize shortly when we begin to focus on micro-level factors, the legislation also places a duty of care on employees. This amounts to a requirement for employees to behave in ways that contribute to health and safety. It is for this reason that we are emphasizing the importance of self-care, resilience and the necessary steps to safeguard ourselves from harm (although not in a victim-blaming way). It is about recognizing that ensuring adequate health and safety is a shared responsibility, as is the responsibility to make sure that we not only survive, but at least also have the potential to thrive.

Toxic organizations

The organizational context also needs to be understood as part of even wider sociopolitical context – for example, in terms of the influence of the current dominance of neoliberal thinking. We have already highlighted that the problems brought about by managerialism have their roots in such thinking.

The incompatibility between free-market ideology and the shrinking of public services does not fit at all well with the harsh realities of trying to work positively in empowering ways with some of the most disadvantaged and vulnerable people in our communities. As we have noted, this places immense pressures on organizations at all levels. One unfortunate consequence of this (largely as a result of the vicious circles that tend to develop) is that organizations can become *toxic*.

Albrecht (2006) explains toxicity in the following terms:

> *Toxic behaviors* ... are those that cause others to feel devalued, inadequate, intimidated, angry, frustrated, or guilty. *Nourishing behaviors* cause others

to feel valued, capable, loved, respected, and appreciated.

(p. xiii)

A toxic organization is one where toxic behaviours not only occur (they may occur at any time in any organization), but also become part of the culture – they come to be normalized. Walton (2008) offers helpful comment:

> a toxic organisation is defined as one within which behaviours which poison, are disruptive, destructive, exploitive, dysfunctional and abusive are pervasive and tolerated. Instances of this would include workplace bullying and harassment in its various forms, deception and fraudulent dealings, the forced imposition of unrealistic workloads and the fostering of disruptive internal competition resulting in bitter and destructive 'turf' battles. In such environments feuding between different departments and functions is likely to lead to a 'blame' culture, embedded patterns of misinformation and misrepresentation, together with the condoning of overly competitive and aggressive interpersonal behaviour.

(pp. 9-10)

While we would not want to overgeneralize, the experience of both authors has led us to conclude that toxic organizations are not uncommon in many sectors of social work. Again, this brings us back to a challenge of leadership, with all members of an organization having some share of the leadership responsibility for addressing toxicity. Of course, the higher up the formal hierarchy we are, the more of a responsibility we have, but cultures are shared entities and therefore shared responsibilities – we all have our part to play.

Micro

As we have already mentioned, one of the features of stressed and overpressurized workplaces is the tendency for vicious circles to develop. And, indeed, this can be seen as an important theme of the book as a whole. One of the vicious circles that is often visible at a micro level is the tendency towards self-disempowerment – that is, the steps that some people take at certain times that have the effect of reducing their power and control, leaving them more open to any adverse aspects of the situation.

Self-disempowerment is a subtle process that most people are unaware of. It is not at all uncommon for people to do themselves down without any awareness that they are doing so. This is often linked to low morale. Just as a person wrestling with depression will often engage in self-undermining (part of a vicious circle that plays a part in sustaining the depression), people immersed in a culture characterized by low morale will often disempower themselves – for example, by allowing cynicism to lead them to give up on various things before they have even tried.

Self-blame

At the root of self-blame are self-doubt and negative self-talk, by which we mean the common tendency to tell ourselves that this is our own fault, that we are letting ourselves and other people down – rather than recognizing and affirming that the wider circumstances are letting us down. It is ironic that, as social workers, we will often be helping people to avoid self-blame by looking more holistically at the situation (for example, challenging the victim of domestic violence to abandon the common idea that they 'deserved it', that they 'let their partner down' in some way), and yet not recognize that we may be adopting the same faulty reasoning ourselves.

This tendency to undermine ourselves (another aspect of self-disempowerment) makes it harder to get through the work pressures, and so this contributes to our struggle. It can be the beginning of the vicious circle, in the sense that the more difficult it is for us to get through the work, the more pressurized we will feel. The more pressurized we feel, the more likely it will be that we will blame ourselves for the circumstances and not look more holistically at the bigger picture. This can undermine our motivation, make us less creative and less able to learn and it will tire us out faster. This can then mean that we adopt a negative or even cynical attitude characterized by defeatism. This can then feed into, or even be the start of, a shared culture of low morale.

Significantly, members of the caring professions tend to be more vulnerable to self-blame because we tend to be 'other directed' – that is, likely to put other people's needs before our own. Understandable though this is, we need to be able to move past this if we are to avoid the harmful contribution of self-blame. We shall return to this topic in Chapter 10.

Vicious circles

We keep coming back to the theme of low morale. Part of the reason for this is that low morale will make it harder to get through the work, and difficulty getting through the work will contribute to low morale, and so it goes on, a very destructive vicious circle indeed. As we noted in Chapter 2, low morale is a highly problematic phenomenon. One particularly destructive aspect of this is that where people withdraw into a sort of bubble of self-doubt, self-blame and negative self-talk. This has the tendency to separate people, drive them apart, rather than bring them together. The net result of this can be a lack of solidarity. We have seen this happen many times in many teams. Just at the point where people should be pulling together and supporting one another, this process of self-disempowerment generates a culture of low morale, negativity and cynicism, which then acts as an obstacle to a collective response and mutual support. This subsequently creates another vicious circle, in so far as a lack of social solidarity and a mutual support ethos makes it harder for everyone to get by, let alone thrive.

This, in turn, can lead to yet another vicious circle. Even the best, most experienced, most competent managers will struggle to address such significant challenges and be able to rectify the problems involved. Consequently, this can lead to a lack of faith in the manager on the part of practitioners, leaving them feeling isolated, unsupported and vulnerable. This can then lead to a process of self-disempowerment on the managers' part. Indeed, this is what many managers have told us – avoiding this cycle of self-disempowerment is extremely difficult in working in a context where some degree of self-disempowerment has become the norm. Consequently, negativity breeds negativity, self-doubt breeds self-doubt, and so on.

Once again, there is no magic answer. However, being aware of the problem and its potentially dire consequences, at least gives us a basis for working together to support one another in challenging these and other aspects of self-disempowerment. Breaking out of vicious circles can be very difficult, as they are self-perpetuating, but the first step needs to be aware of their existence (and the harm they do).

Bullying and harassment

It is unfortunately the case that, in some settings, scenarios like we have described here can lead to bullying behaviour (an example of toxic behaviour, as discussed above). People's frustrations with the nigh-on impossible challenges they appear to be facing can lead to inappropriate responses, including treating colleagues in a less than dignified way – in other words, bullying or harassment (see Thompson, 2019b).

With or without bullying or harassment, the high level of tension in such situations can also be a factor in generating a significant number of conflicts in a team or other work setting. Of course, this can lead to yet another vicious circle whereby the pressures and tensions created by conflict add to the overall level of pressure, potentially leading to harmful stress. And, of course, the more stress there is, the more tension and thus more potential for conflict. The more conflict there is, the more scope for bullying and harassment (bullying and harassment commonly arise from conflicts being badly handled). Round and round these vicious circles go.

Self-care

The implications of all these vicious circles is that we are potentially vulnerable to considerable harm to our well-being and even to our health, and potentially our career overall. It is for this reason that there is such a strong emphasis in this book and in social work generally on the idea of self-care. This is such an important topic that we will explore it in much more detail in Chapter 9. But, for now, we want to make the point that, although the macro-level factors are extremely important and need to be given full attention, they do not tell the whole story. Unfortunately, the way situations evolve at a micro level can intensify and exacerbate the difficulties generated by the macro-level circumstances.

Macro and micro: A holistic approach

We made the point earlier that some people make the mistake of failing to pay attention to the wider circumstances and therefore adopt a perspective that is dangerously narrow, and which potentially contributes to a victim-blaming culture. We also recognized that some people go to the other extreme and focus exclusively on macro-level phenomena, as if what happens at a micro level has no bearing on the reality of people's experiences. Of course, the psychosocial roots of social work should prepare us well for understanding that, to get an adequate understanding of the circumstances, we need to take account of both the macro and the micro issues. Significantly, we also have to be tuned in to the powerful and complex dynamics that operate between the macro and micro. Each can influence the other in subtle and significant ways.

We are all unique individuals, but we are unique individuals in a social context (Thompson, 2021). If we want to have a good appreciation of human experience, then we need to grasp both what is unique about our individual circumstances and what is shared in terms of wider sociological factors, such as cultural and structural elements. What we do, think and feel at a personal, individual level will both reflect and contribute to cultural and structural factors. Those cultural and structural factors will, in turn, play a part in shaping our personal experience. But, to get the full picture, we need to take account of how the personal and the cultural levels interact and influence one another, and how, in turn, the cultural and structural levels interact and influence one another (Thompson, 2018c).

There are (at least) two major implication arising from this. First, we should not place the blame for wider organizational difficulties on the shoulders of managers, as if the problem is simply incompetent managers. This is not to say that there is no such thing as an incompetent manager, but it would be a gross overgeneralization and oversimplification to see the wider organizational problems as purely a matter of personal inadequacy. This is the equivalent of blaming parents who struggle to bring up their children in poverty or other adverse circumstances, a mistake we should be very familiar with as social workers. A non-judgemental attitude is part of the social work value base for a reason. Blaming managers is simply transferring the problem of victim blaming to a different level within the organization. This is not intended as a defence of poor management, but, rather, a recognition that we are dealing with a complex, multilevel phenomenon – a simplistic 'bloody managers' mentality is not helpful.

Second, we should not focus exclusively, or even primarily, on the micro level and thereby feed self-doubt and self-disempowerment. The common tendency for many practitioners to fall back on an 'It's my fault, I'm not up to it' approach to the situation is also not helpful (see the discussion of self-blame in Chapter 10).

It is to be hoped that the discussion here of the complex interplay of various vicious circles will help to present a more sophisticated picture of what is happening when people face such intense pressures that they begin to doubt whether they will be able to survive for much longer (and potentially give up on the hope of ever thriving).

As social workers, we will be aware that, in families, groups and communities, a high level of pressure and tension can lead to people taking out their pressures and frustrations on each other, thereby making the situation worse. We need to apply the same logic to understanding our own circumstances and appreciate that the problem lies in the vicious circles (and the complex array of factors that give rise to them), and thereby resist the temptation to come up with simple answers that either blame others or blame ourselves. Again, it is about being non-judgemental, including towards ourselves.

What can be helpful is to consider reflexive practice. This is part of reflective practice (Thompson and Thompson, 2018). It refers to the ability to reflect on not only the situation we are in, but also our specific role within it. It is about having (or developing) greater self-awareness, in this case awareness of what we are doing (and what is being done to us) at a micro level and what role the macro level is playing in shaping the circumstances.

Our professional experience of working with people and their problems should mean that we are well placed to understand these issues at a theoretical level, but, of course, it can be a different matter when it involves looking at ourselves, our own circumstances and our own reactions to them.

Conclusion

We have noted that there are quite a few macro-level factors that are highly significant and quite a few micro-level ones too. We need to take account of both these sets of factors, not choose between them. We have also emphasized that, to get the full picture, we need to consider the interactions between the macro and the micro. Considering them in isolation will not be enough; we need to incorporate an understanding of the dynamics between the two domains.

How we react to these immense and complex problems involves a set of skills. Consideration of these skills will form the basis of Chapter 5. However, first, we need to be tuned in to what the research base has to say, so that, in taking our efforts forward, we can be as well informed as reasonably possible. Chapter 4 is therefore devoted to a review of some of the main research areas that can cast light on the current state of the social work scene and the myriad pressures involved.

Chapter 4: The Research Base

Introduction

As we have noted, stress is a popular topic with a large literature base, ranging from in-depth academic papers to very superficial articles that are basically little more than marketing copy for some sort of solution that is being offered for sale. Indeed, the 'stress industry' is a huge phenomenon, with products and services that range from legitimate sources of help to all sorts of weird and wonderful 'magical cures' of one type or another.

Much of the popular literature is, as you might expect, superficial and simplistic, often offering misleading information – for example, that stress is good for you or that it can be resolved purely by breathing exercises or other passive coping methods. We should therefore be very critical when taking on board information presented through the popular media or social media. For example, next time you are asked in magazine or on social media to take a test to see how stressed you are, take it with a very large pinch of salt.

Thankfully, we can safely ignore this type of simplistic populism, as we have available to us a significant body of research that can cast significant light on what stress – and workplace problems more broadly – are all about. There is a huge body of published research relating to stress and associated concerns related to the workplace in general, and there is much we can learn from that treasure trove of information. What we also have is a large and growing body of research relating specifically to stress in social work, research that builds on the wider research base but which focuses on some of the aspects of the phenomenon that are specific to social work or play a particularly significant role within social work.

The chapter is divided into four main sections. In the first one we take a brief look at some of the key lessons that the broader body of stress research has made available to us. Next, we narrow our focus down to research that concentrates specifically on stress and related issues in social work. In the third section, we narrow our focus further by examining the working conditions research that BASW and SWU have recently been involved in. Finally, we explore some of the main implications of what this broad research base tells us.

It needs to be borne in mind that the research base we are drawing on is vast and spans a long period of time. This means that the points we make will necessarily be selective and far from comprehensive. There is so much more that could be said about stress research than we can possibly cover in one short chapter.

Overall, then, we do not have to start from scratch or rely solely on our own experience in terms of making sense of stress and associated workplace problems. The research base gives us a good foundation to build on, but, of course, like any research base, it will not tell us everything we need to know.

Stress research in context

There has been a longstanding interest in workplace stress within the academic discipline of psychology and much less in sociology or the other social sciences. Consequently, there has understandably been a stronger focus on the individual's experiences of stress than other aspects, and so we need to bear in mind that the picture presented will often not be as holistic as we would like.

In his discussion of a more relationship-based approach to workplace well-being, Costello (2020) points out that:

> At any given time, a sixth of the population goes to work experiencing the physical (somatic) symptoms of emotional distress – sleep problems, not eating properly, headaches and migraines, neck and back pains, tiredness, and more.

> (p. 5)

The Chartered Institute of Personnel and Development (CIPD), the leading professional organization for people management, add to this picture in reporting the results of their survey:

> Our findings ... show that stress continues to be one of the main causes of short-and long-term absence, particularly in the public sector. A minority of people professionals report their organisation had no stress-related absence

in their organisation over the last 12 months, showing how prevalent work-related stress is in UK workplaces.

(CIPD, 2020, p. 25)

It is clear, then, that stress and associated mental health problems are very much part of the contemporary workplace scene, not just in social work, but across the board, reflecting our comments in Chapter 1 about the changing nature of the workplace.

But, while these problems are very much today's problems, they are by no means new. For example, in the 1970s Kobasa and Maddi (1977) drew on existentialist thought to develop a 'hardiness' model of stress that proved to be very influential. Based on the existentialist notion that, whatever happens to us, we always have choices that we can make, they argued that much will depend on how we react to the pressures we face, the choices we make in trying to manage the demands made on us. This spawned a great deal of research and theorizing premised on the recognition that stress is not simply a matter of the (objective) pressures we face, but also involves our (subjective) reaction to it – specifically in relation to the decisions we make in terms of how to respond. This was not intended to mean that people were responsible for their own stress, although it has often been misinterpreted as such. The point being made was that there is scope for avoiding being the passive victims of the pressures we face.

'Hardiness' was the term used to refer to a person's ability to withstand pressures and thereby keep them within manageable limits. This laid the foundations for the current emphasis on resilience, a topic we shall return to below.

Central to hardiness are the three Cs:

- *Commitment* This refers to having a sense of purpose that enables us to find our work meaningful. By being committed to and engaged in our work we are more likely to be better equipped to cope with the pressures we face. This links well with our view of not losing sight of our professionalism as an important factor to be aware of.

- *Control* We have already commented on the significance of control, in the sense that the more control we have, the less likely we are to have difficulties, we are to become stressed. Organizations that limit people's control and autonomy over their own work are unnecessarily causing problems for their employees and therefore for themselves, as Huq's (2015) work on employee empowerment highlights. For example, procedures that constrain rather than enable can be key factors in generating additional pressures that lead to stress.

- *Challenge* Work that is too easy and undemanding will not motivate us or bring the best out of us. Where our work is suitably challenging, we are more likely to engage with it and get the positives from it. This is clearly something that applies to social work – the challenge of making a positive difference in exceptionally difficult circumstances can play a part in developing that hardiness and, in our experience, that is exactly what happens for most people.

The hardiness approach also chimed well with the work of Lazarus and colleagues (Lazarus and Folkman, 1984) who emphasized the role of 'appraisal' – that is, the way we interpret the pressures we face. For example, one person could interpret being insulted as a minor irritation that causes no distress, while another person could be devastated by the same insult. There will be various psychological (and sociological) reasons that can help to explain such widely different responses to the same basic stimulus.

Collins (2019) makes the important point that we also need to pay attention to the notion of 'the hardy organization' – that is, looking at what can be done at an organizational level and not leaving all the responsibility with individuals. Without doing so, there is a danger that we reinforce a pathological model of stress.

The notion of hardiness can also be seen to underpin the more recent development of interest in resilience as a counterbalance to stress. Waugh (2014) explains the origins of the term:

> The word *resilience* is originally a metallurgical term that characterizes the ability of a metal to be stressed (e.g. bent or twisted) and then to rebound to its original form when that stress is no longer applied.

While this is a useful way of understanding how the term evolved, it needs to be adapted in two ways to apply to living, breathing people, rather than inanimate metals. First, while the person, like a metal, may return to their previous level of functioning, they may have been traumatized by the experience in ways that do not come to the surface until much later – as often happens with children who are abused and experience trauma-related mental health problem in later life (Walsh and Thompson, 2019). And, of course, in line with crisis theory, with humans, there is the scope to not only return to previous functioning, but also actually to grow and learn from the experience and therefore achieve a higher level of functioning.

Second, there are also the sociological aspects to consider. Unlike metals, people's experiences are strongly influenced by the social context. Whether a person 'rebounds to their original form' will depend on a number of sociological factors, not least the level and quality of support they receive. So, while the metallurgy analogy is helpful up to a point, it also has significant limitations.

A key element of resilience is the ability to adapt our emotional responses to suit the situation we are in. Waugh captures the point in the following terms:

> research suggests that resilient people are characterized by the co-occurrence of positive and negative emotions in stressful situations (Folkman & Moskowitz, 2000; Ong, Bergeman, Biscontin, & Wallace, 2006), and that this co-occurrence may be due to the ability of resilient people to flexibly adapt their emotional responses to match the demands of the situation (Waugh, Thompson, & Gottlib, 2011; Westphal, Seivert, & Bonnano, 2010).
>
> (2014, p. 73)

The idea that positive emotions can exist alongside negative ones fits with our earlier discussions of the dangers of allowing a culture of negativity and defeatism to squeeze out positives and leave us with a dangerously unbalanced approach to our work and to our life.

However, one problem with Waugh's approach which reflects a common view of resilience is his use of the term 'resilient people', as if there are two categories of people, those who are resilient and those who are not. This neglects the situational and sociological aspects of resilience – for example, the family context which can either nurture or stifle resilience (Rosenblatt, 2020). A much more holistic approach to resilience is called for if we are to avoid it contributing to pathologizing people whose personal or social circumstances act as a barrier to resilience.

This fits with the strengths perspective that has proven to be influential in recent years (Desai, 2018; Saleebey, 2012). The tendency for a focus on the negatives to squeeze out consideration of the positives can produce a distorted picture of the situation. This can apply directly to social work practice (in terms of the need for a balanced assessment that includes strengths, for example) as well as to efforts to keep stress at bay (by making sure that we take account of the strengths and values that sustain us as well as the problems and pressures that we face).

This brings us back to the importance of meaning making. Park and Slattery (2014) draw on a range of research studies to offer an understanding of stress (and especially trauma) as 'meaning violation' – that is, distress caused by an experience that requires us to re-evaluate our worldview or framework of meaning. This is consistent with the research of Neimeyer and colleagues (2009) which seeks to explain complicated grief as a crisis in meaning. Both these approaches chime well with our own view of stress and surviving as spiritual matters in view of the key role of meaning in shaping our experiences and our understanding of them. That is, we can understand pressures as a spiritual challenge, stress as a spiritual diminishment, survival as spiritual renewal and thriving as spiritual flourishing. Park and Slattery echo our emphasis on spirituality:

> Existential concerns regarding control, identity, relationships, and meaning are frequently raised by illness and loss (Cole & Pargament, 1999). Spiritual issues are often embedded in these existential questions, and spirituality may be a resource promoting healing. Pargament and his colleagues have developed several interventions that help people draw on spirituality as a resource for recovery.
>
> (2014, p. 278)

Part of spirituality is 'connectedness', the sense of being part of something bigger than ourselves. Trade unions can be seen to be part of this, in the sense that they bring so many people together with a common sense of purpose. Not surprisingly, research suggests that people working in unionized settings experience less stress. Costello (2020, p. 11), drawing on the work of Haile *et al.* (2015) which suggests that unionized workers show higher levels of job satisfaction and well-being. As Costello puts it: '*Trade unions* are shown to improve workplace wellbeing through a civilising process that mediates organisational change, improves pay, and working conditions etc.' (Bryson *et al.*, 2013).

Research specific to social work

Research on stress in social work is by no means a new phenomenon. For example, in the 1990s there was a Stress in Social Work Research Group that produced a much-cited article (Thompson *et al.*, 1996) and other resources, but these works were by no means the first.

Collins (2019) summarizes some of the key studies of stress in social work:

> Causes of stress for social workers are seen as many and varied. They have been well documented in various large scale surveys. For instance, in the UK a Community Care study indicated concerns about work conditions, the quality of supervision, lack of support for decisions made, size of caseloads, and lack of promotion prospects (Mickel, 2009). In 2015 another survey revealed very high levels of stress with very high percentages of workers thinking of leaving their jobs and leaving social work (Schraer, 2015). An extensive study by McFadden (2016) found high levels of emotional exhaustion amongst almost all social work practitioners, while two thirds experienced depersonalisation – a lack of feeling, lack of empathy, and uncaring responses. High levels of exhaustion were reported for all levels of caseload, even for smaller caseloads and for those who received supportive supervision.
>
> (p. 9)

He goes on to provide example after example of studies that highlight concerning levels of pressure and stress among a wide range of social work groups. However, an important theme in his work around stress over a number of years has been the need to counterbalance the negatives with the positives – for example, the consistently reported high levels of job satisfaction (Cooper, 2015). This has echoes of our comments earlier about the need to recognize that positive feelings can exist alongside negative ones without the latter squeezing out the former.

Clearly, then, there is a strong research base that gives clear messages that problems of stress are not uncommon in social work. However, we also have to recognize that there is another side to this story: there are positives, there are strategies for coping and, as Collins emphasizes, there is always hope. We would also add that there is always the empowering potential of resilience – rooted in solidarity – in the face of adversity.

The working conditions research

It was in the context of the recognition of stress and the need for solidarity in dealing with the challenges it brings that SWU and BASW decided to see what could be done to address the situation. Consequently, a partnership was set up involving SWU, BASW and experienced and renowned researcher, Dr Jermaine Ravalier, from Bath Spa University. This partnership has so far spawned two important research reports and a toolkit, and more research involving the International Federation of Social Workers is underway at the time of writing. The focus of this research has been working conditions and their relationship with stress.

The toolkit that emerged from this partnership summarizes the situation as follows:

> Over the past two years Dr Jermaine Ravalier and colleagues from Bath Spa University have worked with BASW and SWU to conduct two of the largest surveys of social worker wellbeing and working conditions in the UK (Ravalier, 2019; Ravalier et al., 2020) which together had over 5000 respondents.
> Using a methodology that had been used with other public sector professionals, the research identified where problems in working conditions impact negatively on social worker stress and wellbeing.

The research was structured around the Health and Safety Executive's seven management standards in relation to stress:

- Demands;
- Control;
- Managerial support;
- Peer support;
- Relationships;
- Role; and
- Change.

The first of the two studies concluded that:

> Results demonstrate high levels of turnover intentions, presenteeism and low job satisfaction. Regression analyses found that the interaction between high demands, low levels of control and poor managerial support was related to social worker stress and related outcomes. Qualitative content analysis of the open-ended question corroborated and extended these findings, also demonstrating that poor ergonomic set-up of the work environment and a blame culture were adding to the experience of stress.
>
> (Ravalier, 2019, p. 371)

The second study also raised concerns about the significance of stress in modern social work:

> results demonstrated poor working conditions, irrespective of job role, and regression analysis suggested each of demands, control, managerial support, role and change influenced stress. Qualitative results found that workload, lack of managerial support, and service user/family abuse were distinct demands associated with the role, whereas buffering positive resources were: the social work role, peer support, and positive managerial support.
>
> (Ravalier et al., 2020)

Both these studies indicate that there is much to be concerned about in the contemporary social work world. However, there is also much to be positive about, as we have seen, in terms of the value of what we do in social work as significant contributors to a humane society, our professionalism, our (potential for) solidarity and, of course, the problem-solving skills that are at the heart of our practice.

One of the main benefits of the working conditions research projects has been to emphasize the wider context of stress and thereby move us away from the stigmatizing stereotype of a person experiencing stress as someone who is weak or inadequate. It helps to reinforce the point that we need to adopt a holistic approach that offers a fuller understanding as a basis for empowerment, not an individualistic one that pathologizes and disempowers.

What does the research base tell us?

For research to be of value we need a balanced approach to how we consume it. At one extreme, there will be people who disregard research evidence, especially if it challenges their worldview or threatens their vested interests. For example, there is no shortage of examples of politicians who have commissioned research at considerable expense, only to disregard it if the results do not fit with their ideology in general or their particular plans at that time. At the other extreme, there are people who are highly deferential towards research and the academic world in general and who will therefore never question research findings or try to fit them into a wider picture.

In between these two unhelpful extremes lies critical thinking. That is, we should not reject research just because it does not fit with our preconceptions (we would never learn the lessons of research if we adopted such an approach), but nor should we take on board research without first critically evaluating it. This means applying our critical faculties to look at who funded the research, what premises does it take for granted (and are these valid), and whether the conclusions logically follow from the data generated. Achieving this balance enables us to learn from what the research has to offer, but without being led astray by unsound or misleading research.

With this in mind, we can begin to look at the lessons that can be drawn out from the research to date on stress in general and stress in social work in particular. Once again, we need to be realistic in terms of what we can cover in the space available. We shall therefore limit ourselves to what we see as three key 'messages':

1. *Stress is multidimensional*

The simplistic idea that stress is the consequence of someone not being able to 'cut it' in a pressurized set of circumstances is far from the truth. Such a view fails to do justice to the complex dynamics that give rise to stress. It also adds to the problem by stigmatizing stress and thereby discouraging people from asking for support precisely at the time they need it most. Costello (2020) captures the point well:

> People who experience stress at work are seen as weak, having some character flaw or lacking backbone. Thinking of stress in this way is inappropriate and potentially dangerous. It forces the issue underground for some, and promotes a culture of shame in others that gets in the way of people either asking for help, or taking time off to get better.
>
> (p. 5)

What this tells us, then, is that we need a strong and sustained campaign to challenge the idea that stress is purely an individual problem best dealt with by therapeutic interventions aimed at strengthening the resolve of the individual employee. Such a narrow perspective pays little or no attention to the wider macro-level factors that will often prove to be highly significant.

This is why we have been advocating a holistic approach that looks at the whole picture and thereby avoids the dangerous distortions of considering only the micro-level issues. As we noted in Chapter 3, if we want to make any progress in terms of addressing the problems presented by stress, we need to address not only the micro-level factors, but also the macro-level ones and, indeed, the interactions between the two levels.

It can be helpful to think in terms of a *well-being interventions continuum*. At the individual level we would need to think about ways of helping, supporting and empowering people in terms of the challenges they are facing – for example, guidance on prioritizing and other such interventions designed to avoid – or break out of – vicious circles. At the other extreme would be organizational interventions, such as the removal of a blame culture, initiatives to stamp out institutional racism and other forms of discrimination and similar whole-organization steps. In between, at what we might call the 'meso' level would be intermediate interventions, such as team initiatives and/or cultural changes at the team or section level.

Interventions that are limited to the individual or micro level are not only likely to be far less effective, but also run the risk of being counterproductive. Looking holistically at the full range of interventions is therefore the wise way forward.

It is important to emphasize that challenging an overreliance on individualistic approaches does not mean that such methods have no value (they can – and do – have a role to play, provided that they are part of a wider repertoire and not the only tool in the box). Nor does it mean that we should contribute to a 'reverse blame' culture – that is, one where it is simplistically assumed that all responsibility for workplace problems lies at the door of the organization or its management team. As we have seen, stress arises from complex multidimensional dynamics and cannot be pinned down to one simple cause.

Again, Costello (2020) casts helpful light on this:

> Organisations are not wholly responsible for the stress we experience at work. It is too simplistic to attach the blame to either the individual or the faceless monolith. Instead, stress has to be understood in terms of a multi-layered physiological, social and political phenomenon.
>
> (p. 8)

To this we would want to add psychological (especially emotional) and spiritual dimensions.

It is therefore fair to say that the research base cautions us against adopting too narrow, simple and fixed a view of what is happening when someone shows signs of stress

2. Stress has many costs

Even a cursory look at the stress research quickly highlights the fact that stress is a costly feature of working life. Sickness absence rates, staff turnover rates, losses in productivity and so on are widely reported. The human costs, of course, are much more difficult to measure, but are none the less highly visible in a number of ways.

So, when people say that stress is good for you, whether deliberately in an attempt to distract attention from organizational failings or unintentionally due to being unenlightened about such matters, they are masking the significant costs associated with stress.

Bill Jordan, one of social work's most esteemed and respected authors, distinguishes between the material economy and the interpersonal economy, the latter being where social work can really make an impact:

> The difference between the material economy producing goods, and the interpersonal economy producing feelings (including, morale, team spirit and solidarity) and culture (ideas, images, science, art, music and drama) is that the latter produces something intangible and difficult to measure. But what the interpersonal economy produces is *real*.
>
> (2007, p. xi)

Stress can therefore be understood to have significant costs associated with it in terms of the interpersonal economy. It can drive people apart, create unnecessary conflicts and tensions, reduce morale and generally reduce the quality of life of the people affected.

In a very real sense, social work is about stress. What we mean by this is that so much of what we do is about preventing, alleviating or removing other people's stress. It is therefore both unfortunate and ironic that stress should have become such a major problem for our own working lives and beyond.

3. Stress is not inevitable

One particularly significant and worrying development in recent years is that stress has become normalized, in the sense that it has now become so prevalent that people have come to expect to be stressed. Once again, we need to revisit the key distinction between pressure and stress. Pressure is what we are paid to deal with, but stress is where that pressure has reached a level that it is harming us. Where this occurs, it is potentially a breach of health and safety legislation, as employers are called upon to protect their staff from undue hazards in the workplace – and that includes stress. We have to be very clear that being under pressure – even a great deal of pressure – is perfectly normal and legitimate, but when that pressure reaches unmanageable and harmful levels and becomes stress, it is no longer legitimate and should not therefore be seen as normal.

Social work, by its very nature, is a pressurized job, but it is not necessarily a stressful one – it is various other factors, both micro and macro, that can mean we may cross the line between harmless pressure and harmful stress.

Once again, Costello (2020) makes apt comment:

> Organisations content to promote "Mental Health Awareness" seem all too blind to the ways they may contribute to creating the *abnormal circumstances* that negatively affect their employees, and instead assume that stress is inevitable, good for you, and only affects those lacking in resilience. None of this is true: every vase ultimately overflows when too much water is poured into it.
>
> (p. 6)

This brings us back to the need for balance. Pathologizing the individual by adopting a narrow, individualistic approach that neglects the significance of the wider social and organizational context is clearly not the path we would want to follow, although, sadly, it is the default setting for a lot of people and a lot of organizations. However, going to the other extreme by assuming that the problem lies purely at a wider level and therefore there is nothing individuals can do will feed a sense of hopelessness and helplessness that can trigger one or more vicious circles. There is indeed much we can do, especially at a team level where the quality and quantity of support on offer can make all the difference.

Before leaving the subject of research and its significance, there are two points we need to highlight. First, when using research relating to stress, we need to be aware of the problem of definition and self-reporting. For example, if the research is not clear about what is meant by stress (as opposed to non-harmful pressure), many respondents will say they are stressed when what they mean is that they are under pressure that they are actually managing to cope with.

Second, it needs to be remembered that any type of research needs to be *interpreted*. The facts generally do not speak for themselves; they need to be filtered through a conceptual framework to make sense of them – that is, they need to be theorized. This does not mean that research data cannot be relied upon, but it does mean that we need to approach it critically, trying to find the balance we mentioned before between dismissing research and accepting it uncritically.

Conclusion

As we pointed out at the beginning of this chapter, the research base is so vast that we cannot possibly do justice to it all in the limited space available. However, we are confident that you will feel that what we have been able to cover will be helpful in broadening and deepening your understanding of workplace challenges in general and stress in particular. We very much hope that this additional understanding will be not only of academic interest to you, but also of practical value in attempting to rise to workplace challenges in an informed way.

Research is, of course, closely associated with science and rationality and, in many ways, that is a clear strength in terms of the reliability and validity of the information good-quality research generates. However, what even the best qualitative research cannot fully capture is the lived experience of being under stress and the emotional challenges involved in that. It is therefore important that, while we take on board (with due critical scrutiny) what the research base has to tell us, we should not make the mistake of assuming that the testimony of practitioners' (and managers') experience on a day-to-day basis has nothing valid to tell us.

We also need to return to our themes of spirituality and meaning making. Research is a form of storytelling, a set of narratives that can aid our understanding (or distort our understanding if the methodology was not rigorous enough). By balancing what the research has to tell us with the lessons to be learned from our own life experiences, we can build a picture that should be able to help us to plan how best to identify and address the problems stress brings, so that we can support one another in moving forward positively.

As with this book as a whole, the research base does not offer magic answers or formula solutions. However, what it should do is offer us a better grasp of the complexities involved while also highlighting which aspect of the subject matter we still have little understanding of. In this way, good research should not only aid us in tackling real-life problems in practice, but also act as the seeds for further research.

Chapter 5: Self-management Skills

Introduction

In his book on authentic leadership, Neil Thompson makes the key point that however limiting the situation we are in may be, there are always choices to be made (Thompson, 2016a) and those choices will have consequences. This is helpful in enabling us to appreciate the significance of self-management skills as a key aspect of going from surviving to thriving, as we are constantly making choices.

As was emphasized in Chapter 3, we need to look at both the macro and micro. Self-management skills clearly come under the heading of the micro level, but this is not to say that macro-level issues do not have a part to play. Once again, we need a holistic perspective that looks at the big picture.

The challenge we face is being able to operate effectively as professionals within highly constrained and often unhelpful organizational and sociopolitical circumstances. This is quite a significant challenge, in so far as social work is difficult enough (intrinsic pressures) without the added pressures arising from the current sociopolitical situation we have been outlining (extrinsic pressures). The combination of these two sets of pressures presents us with quite a formidable undertaking, hence the need for us to be: (i) on our mettle when it comes to attempting to rise to these challenges; and (ii) prepared to support each other as fully as possible. For (i), read optimal self-management skills, and for (ii), read solidarity.

The emphasis in this chapter is therefore on the steps that we can take to optimize our ability to achieve positive outcomes as far as reasonably possible in very difficult circumstances, partly by developing our self-management skills as far as possible and partly by contributing to a culture of support and solidarity. These are complex issues, and so we are not offering any sort of straightforward formula approach that would not do justice to those complexities.

It is important to clarify once again that this is not an exercise in victim blaming.

In fact, we are confident that the issues discussed in this chapter can help to highlight the inadequacies in working conditions and other macro-level factors, as highlighted in Chapters 3 and 4. It is the dynamic (or set of dynamics) between the micro and the macro that is crucial, as is the case in our direct social work practice, of course.

The chapter is in six sections. In the first we focus on some key issues involved in the challenges of managing a high level of pressure. In the second we discuss the significance of change and the role it can play in increasing our pressures. We then move on to explore what is involved in managing people, how to optimize our effectiveness in working alongside others. Fourth, we consider the popular notion of positive thinking.

Next, we explore some issues related to self-management itself, highlighting its importance and offering some guidance on how to practise it effectively. Finally, we consider the significance of self-leadership to see what is involved in having a sense of purpose and direction as a basis for our self-management skills in particular and moving from surviving to thriving more broadly.

Managing pressures

We have already established that, by its very nature, social work is a highly *pressurized* job, but it does not need to be *stressful*. Whether or not it is a source of harmful stress will depend on a number of factors at both the macro and micro levels. Unfortunately, the skills, tools and techniques involved in managing a heavy workload and the associated high levels of pressure have tended not to feature strongly in most aspects of social work education and training. It is as if it is assumed that being able to manage a heavy workload is something that will simply come naturally to people.

Because of this singular significant gap, many people have found themselves struggling to manage pressures because they have not had the opportunity to explore what is involved in effective pressure management. For many years, Neil ran a one-day course on time and workload management for social workers and others. The feedback was consistently very positive, but what was particularly significant was that participants commonly expressed annoyance that they had not been taught about these matters as part of their basic training. They were realizing that there are ways and means of managing pressure more effectively that the course had taught them that they could have benefited from at a much earlier stage in their career. (The course is now available in an e-learning format – see p. 217.)

What has also been unhelpful is that, in many quarters, especially in the business world, there has been an emphasis on *time* management, with considerable resources having been made available for training in this area. This is despite the fact that there is only limited evidence that such an approach is effective in more than a minimal way. There has tended to be too much of an emphasis on the minutiae of managing the workload – for example, tips around how to save a minute or two here and there. We are critical of such approaches because they miss the significant point that time cannot be managed. Time ticks away, whether we like it or not. Of course, we can manage time in the sense of managing a diary, but there is much, much more to managing our pressures than this.

What needs to be managed is the set of demands upon us, the pressures. As we shall see below, this entails a degree of self-management – that is, how effective we are in a number of ways, not least:

- Making sure that time is not wasted as a result of lacking focus or 'drifting';
- Staying as motivated as we can (see below); and
- Using our negotiation skills to prevent ourselves from becoming overloaded.

The traditional focus on time management has therefore tended to oversimplify some complex issues. It has also tended to reinforce a pathologizing model in which anyone who is struggling to cope with the pressures is deemed to be failing because of their lack of effective time management.

Indeed, it is sadly the case that in some work settings time management training can be used punitively, in the sense that some insensitive managers can adopt the view that, because the practitioner has been on a time management training course, they can be given a significantly higher workload. What is often missing from time management training is the recognition that there is a limit to how effective anyone can be – we all have a line between what is a manageable level of pressure and what is an unmanageable level (and therefore a source of stress). The 'last straw' analogy is very applicable here. It can sometimes be just one small additional task or demand that results in that line being crossed. What causes that crossing may be small, but the consequences of it can be of major proportions in terms of the adverse effect on health, well-being and our ability to get our work done.

This leads us into a highly significant point, namely the need to recognize that overloading staff with too much work is actually counterproductive. Where levels of pressure are manageable, employees can be highly productive. However, once the level of pressure reaches the point where it is unmanageable, the ironic consequence is that the worker becomes less productive than before. This will be because an excessive level of pressure will lead to a higher error rate, less creativity, less ability to learn and improve practice, more sickness absence, potentially more conflict and other related difficulties. In short, overloading the employee will serve to reduce productivity, not increase it. In addition to the reduced productivity, there will also, of course, be the human costs to consider, and those could be potentially very significant indeed.

Those human costs are not restricted to the individual(s) concerned. For example, where someone becomes stressed as a result of being overstretched, there can be adverse consequences for their colleagues, their families and their friends. These adverse effects can then have a knock-on effect for wider circles of people. Someone who is stressed may struggle to be an effective parent. A child who is not receiving parental care and attention may express their distress through behaviour that causes problems for others.

It is important to return to the theme of vicious circles because they can be just as significant here as elsewhere. For example, one of the consequences of excessive pressure will often be a reduction in creativity. People who are feeling overwhelmed are likely to withdraw into their security bubble and focus on just surviving. This narrowing of perspective runs counter to the breadth of vision that is needed for a creative approach. There is a significant irony here, in so far as one of the most effective ways of managing a high level of pressure is to be creative, reflecting the adage that necessity is the mother of invention.

Pink (2018) draws a distinction between two types of work: algorithmic and heuristic. The former refers to types of work that are highly routinized and require little or no need to think about what is involved – it is simply a matter of following a set pattern or procedure. Working in a fast-food restaurant would be an example of this. Heuristic work, by contrast, involves having to think things through, to test out ideas and try different ways of moving forward and getting the job done. Clearly, social work fits more into the latter category than the former.

This raises two important issues. First, we can note how managerialism, with its emphasis on targets and proceduralization, has created problems (and contributed to stress) by trying to fit social work (and other public services) more into the former category – another example of trying to fit a square peg into a round hole.

Second, the more algorithmic our work becomes, the less scope there is for creative problem solving. Algorithmic work relies on a narrow focus, while creative problem solving requires us to think more broadly in order to identify ways forward that would not otherwise have been apparent to us. Creativity involves looking at situations from different perspectives, while an algorithmic approach is based on maintaining the same narrow perspective. Because excessive pressure tends to have the effect of increasing anxiety, there will generally be a defensive narrowing of focus, a greater reliance on algorithmic working (people who are burnt out tend to become highly algorithmic) and thus less creativity.

As Hamer (2007) points out: 'If our own creativity is stifled, then it becomes difficult to foster the creativity in others that encourages them to pursue the kinds of lives they hope to have' (p. ix). Consequently, the less creative we are, the less effective and productive we will be, and consequently the more pressurized we will feel. Given the significance of relationships and interpersonal interactions as a basis for social work, clearly an algorithmic approach based on mindless routines will be highly problematic (see the discussion of 'Human Connection' in Thompson, 2018a).

Avoiding crossing that line from a manageable level of pressure to an unmanageable one is therefore crucial. Before the line is crossed, creativity can be an excellent advantage and significant resource. However, once people cross the line into stress territory by reaching the point where their workload is unmanageable, creativity becomes much more difficult to achieve and therefore much less likely to feature as a way of managing pressure. Where organizations encourage their staff to be more creative, this makes perfect sense in the context of a manageable level of pressure, but where the context is one of excessive pressure, such pleas are likely to fall on stony ground and may actually add to the pressures, thereby potentially creating yet another vicious circle.

We do not have space for a fully detailed analysis of what is involved in terms of effective management of pressure, but our discussions in later chapters should be helpful in developing more confident and skilful approaches to managing the combination of workplace and home pressures.

Managing change

The only constant is change is a commonly heard cliché, but it is not too far from the truth. However, Thompson (2013a) makes the important point that the significance of change is generally oversimplified. This applies in at least two main ways:

1. The actual extent of change tends to be overestimated. Even at times of significant change, for every change that is occurring, there will be many more things that are staying the same. We tend to focus on what is new and different and take for granted most of the stuff that is remaining largely the same. This can lead people to panic about change and feel overwhelmed by it.

2. It is commonly assumed that 'people do not like change', but this oversimplifies a much more complex picture. What makes it complex is that much will depend on: (i) the nature of the change (for example, how many people would 'not like change' if the change were a substantial rise in their salary?); and (ii) how effectively or otherwise the change is managed (by the people bringing about and/or trying to manage the change and by ourselves). The approach to managing change will either increase or decrease the pressures arising from the change.

Part of how the change is managed organizationally will depend on the culture. As Ballat and Campling (2011) explain:

Any change, especially imposed from 'outside', is emotionally disruptive and can affect the way people think about their work, their colleagues, their patients and themselves. Most staff are attached to their job and particular ways of working. They invest valued parts of themselves, often at personal cost, and take pride in what their particular service offers. They have found ways of managing their difficult feelings, ways that have become intimately entwined with the way things have been done. A culture where the focus is always on newness leaves people feeling insecure, undervalued and sometimes abandoned. If their service is cut or redesigned, they will feel bereaved, even if they can understand the reasons for the change.

(p. 134)

This passage raises a number of important issues, but we wish to focus on two in particular. First, we have the idea that a culture focusing on newness will generate feelings of insecurity. Unfortunately, many organizations (most?) have tended to try and cope with the immense pressures brought about by neoliberal thinking and managerialist practices by restructuring (in many cases doing so several times). Not surprisingly, many critics have labelled this approach rearranging the deckchairs on the Titanic, as it makes no difference to the underlying problems.

Of course, one of the risks that senior management teams run in engaging in such disruptive wholesale changes is that they add significant pressures on their staff and potentially alienate them by reducing their trust in, and commitment to, the organization, while making little or no positive difference by creating the upheaval in the first place.

Second, there is the recognition that significant change will generally instil a sense of loss and therefore give risk to a grief reaction. Grief is difficult enough to deal with when we know we are grieving, but if we do not realize that we are grieving, the added confusion and distress can be significant.

When it comes to self-management skills, then, we need to think carefully about how we manage change in general and how we deal with the grief issues in particular. As with other aspects of self-management skills, there are no simple answers, but much can be gained by: (i) keeping change in perspective (recognizing that, for everything that is new and different, there will be much that stays familiar and safe); (ii) balancing positives and negatives from any particular change and not just focusing on the negatives; and (iii) not losing sight of solidarity – we should be supporting one another in getting through changes as effectively and productively as possible.

Managing people

How we relate to other people on a day-to-day basis can be highly significant in terms of managing pressures, in the sense that people can be a source of immense support, reassurance, affirmation and validation (hence our emphasis on solidarity). However, they can also be a source of considerable additional pressure – for example, as a result of conflict, a failure on our part to do what we have promised to do, and other such human failings. Sartre (2000) famously argued that 'hell is other people', by which he meant that other people trying to do what they want to do (their 'projects', as he called them) will so often get in the way of what we are trying to do. Other people, then, are a mixed blessing – wonderful and woeful, awesome and awful. To what extent the negatives prevail will depend on how skilful or otherwise we are at handling our interactions with others and bringing about the positives.

Managing pressure therefore depends to a large extent on our effectiveness in managing people. We are therefore using this phrase 'managing people' not in its narrow sense of carrying out human resource duties as a manager, but in the wider sense of managing our day-to-day interactions with other people. A key part of this is managing expectations – that is, making sure that other people's expectations of us are neither unclear nor unrealistic, as both of these can lead to stress. One important technique for negotiating expectations is what is known as 'setting out your stall'. What this means is giving people a clear message what you can and cannot do, what timescales are realistic and what their part in making things happen needs to be.

It is also very wise to establish this right from the outset of our dealings with any particular individual or group of people. Setting out your stall means you are leaving the other people involved in the situation with no doubt about the boundaries of your involvement. If there is any conflict or contradiction in terms of what they expect of you and what you can realistically offer, it is best to identify this and tackle it sooner rather than later. Allowing people to have unrealistic expectations of you is a recipe for ill feeling and an obstacle to partnership-based working. It does not help anyone to allow unrealistic expectations to arise or to go unchallenged if they do arise.

Some people, it would seem, struggle with this, in so far as they appear to lack the assertiveness skills necessary to carry out such negotiations. It is as if their anxiety is such that they do not feel sufficiently comfortable in establishing realistic boundaries around what their contribution to the situation can be. Getting past such obstacles is therefore a necessary part of keeping our pressures within manageable limits. In some social work situations, it is also important that we are sufficiently assertive to make appropriate use of the authority that comes with our role – for example, in safeguarding work and/or mental health statutory duties.

Assertiveness is also important when it comes to our relationship with our managers. It is often the case that managers have no way of knowing (unless you say so) what is an unreasonable level of work for you. Sadly, we have come across many circumstances where one or more practitioners have found themselves in considerable difficulties because their manager unwittingly placed them in a situation of work overload, but they did not take the opportunity to voice their concerns or ask for support. For example, we have come across people who have reached the point where they have become physically ill as a result of stress, people who had supportive managers who would have been more than happy to be very supportive if they had been made aware how serious the problem was.

This raises two important sets of issues. First, it takes us back to the issue of health and safety legislation and the recognition that employees have a duty of care towards themselves in addition to the duty of care owed to them by their employers. It is therefore essential that any concerns about work overload are communicated effectively, and preferably sooner rather than later. For the system to work, people who are experiencing difficulties have to be prepared to raise their concerns and ask for support, while managers need to use their leadership skills to nurture cultures that make it clear that asking for help will not be seen as a sign of weakness or stigmatized in any other way.

Second, the dominant discourse of stress as a sign of a weak individual can make many people reluctant to highlight any concerns they may have about their workload. It can discourage them from communicating about levels of pressure, with the result that they are not sufficiently assertive in establishing where the boundary lies between a manageable level of pressure and an unmanageable one, between one that allows for effective healthy working practices and one that contributes to unhealthy destructive stress. We shall return later to the subject of assertiveness, but for now we simply wish to emphasize the importance of learning how to 'manage your manager'. Some highly skilled managers seem to have a sixth sense in terms of being able to pick up subtle signals at an early stage that indicate that an employee is under too much pressure, but such people tend to be in the minority. For the most part, it is essential that we feel comfortable enough to be able to raise concerns, individually and collectively, when there is a danger that levels of pressure are reaching the point of harm.

Another aspect of managing people is being an effective team member. It is commonly assumed that the person responsible for managing the team is the team manager or equivalent. However, Thompson (2013b) makes the important point that, for a team to achieve maximum effectiveness, it is necessary for all members to contribute to the management of the team. Indeed, expecting the team manager to be successful in leading the team without the cooperation of members is simply to set that person up to fail. What is significant is the attitude of team members towards their role within the team. For example, some people take a passive approach, sit back and allow others to shape the direction, ethos and culture within the team. Others play a more active role in playing a part in trying to ensure that the team dynamics are positive and the culture is a healthy one in which people are supported to learn and grow, develop and thrive, rather than a restrictive one that feeds tension, low morale and potentially stress. Consequently one important question to ask yourself is this: How positive a role are you playing in trying to make sure that the team or workgroup that you are a part of functions well and is a source of support and affirmation, rather than a further set of pressures? One of the themes of this book is the need to think collectively as well as individually, to recognize the importance of solidarity.

Staying positive

Positive psychology has gained a considerable popular following in recent years, despite being heavily criticized in various quarters (for example, Ehrenreich, 2009; Coyne and Tennen, 2010). Hedges (2010) adds to the voices of dissent:

> There is a dark, insidious quality to the ideology promoted by the positive psychologists. They condemn all social critics and iconoclasts, the dissidents and individualists, for failing to surrender and seek fulfilment in the collective lowing of the corporate herd. They strangle creativity and moral autonomy. They seek to mold and shape individual human beings into a compliant collective. The primary teaching of this movement, which reflects the ideology of the corporate state, is that fulfilment is to be found in complete and total social conformity, a conformity that all totalitarian and authoritarian structures seek to impose on those they dominate. Its false promise of harmony and happiness only increases internal anxiety and feelings of inadequacy. The nagging undercurrents of alienation and the constant pressure to exhibit a false enthusiasm and buoyancy destroy real relationships. The loneliness of a work life where self-presentation is valued over authenticity and one must always be upbeat and positive, no matter what one's actual mood or situation, is disorientating and stressful.
>
> (pp. 138-9)

This passage speaks to social work in recognizing that 'looking on the bright side' does not fit neatly with the complexities of distress, trauma, pain, suffering, discrimination, oppression, marginalization and abuse. Focusing on the positives of life is not the same as positive thinking. We can have a balanced approach that considers both the positives and the negatives and adopts a positive, constructive, empowering approach to the whole picture, not just the positives.

This is not to say that positive psychology has nothing to offer. Rather, it is a matter of counselling against uncritically getting on the bandwagon and thereby failing to recognize the emotional complexities involved.

Staying positive is an important idea in social work, given that we have repeatedly emphasized the problems associated with negativity and defeatism. But, being positive and embracing positive psychology uncritically are two different things.

Staying positive, in the sense that we are using it here is about making sure that we do not succumb to the dangers of being dragged down by the intensity and emotional demands of our work or the frustrations of the wider sociopolitical context of neoliberalism. It is, as we have been emphasizing, a matter of doing the best we can in difficult circumstances, rather than allowing negativity to make a bad situation worse.

So often in social work we will encounter people who are in despair or struggling to avoid its clutches, while also having our own battle against hopelessness because of the major challenges we face in the current climate. Collins (2019) reminds us that hope is an important feature of social work. Little can be achieved without hope.

Dreyfus (2012) draws on existentialist thought to establish that despair is more than sadness, regret or disappointment:

> despair exhibits what Kierkegaard calls "the dialectic of eternity." If you are sad, you know that it is temporary. Even if something so terrible happens to you that you feel that you were happy once but that whatever happened makes it impossible for you ever to be happy again, that is certainly misery, but it is not despair. Despair is the feeling that life isn't working for you and, given the kind of person you are, it is impossible for things to work for you; that a life worth living is, in your case, literally impossible.
>
> (p. 102)

Staying positive, then, is not about blind optimism. It is about recognizing the negatives while adopting a positive attitude, rooted in hope and some degree of determination, to counterbalance those negatives. In this way, we are being adversaries of negativity, not victims of it, but nor are we making the mistake of focusing on positives as if the negatives do not exist. Once again, this is where solidarity has a role to play – being part of a positive group is much easier than being positive in isolation

Self-management

It may strike you as strange that the title of this chapter is self-management, and yet so far we have focused on managing pressures, managing change, managing people and staying positive, rather than managing ourselves. However, what we need to recognize is that managing pressures, change and people and staying positive are, in fact, underpinned by self-management. This is because how well we manage pressures will depend to a large extent on how we manage ourselves, how well-organized we are, how focused we are, how motivated we can manage to stay, and how well we keep in touch with our values – the values that sustain us through the difficulties and help us to survive. The technical term for this is self-efficacy.

Self-image refers to how we see ourselves, the model of self that we come to accept. Self-esteem refers to the extent to which we value ourselves and is therefore very significant in terms of our level of confidence. The third element of selfhood, in this regard, is the extent to which we manage ourselves effectively, hence the notion of self-efficacy.

Think of the various people you know and consider how good at self-management each of them is. Who do you see as having a high level of self-efficacy? What can you learn from them? Who do you see as people who struggle with self-efficacy? What can you learn from how they struggle and the mistakes they make?

Once again, we are not indulging in victim blaming by trying to suggest that the answer to the problems of work overload is better self-management. Rather, what we are saying is that difficulties in self-management are likely to make a bad situation worse and trigger one or more vicious circles. But, what is also important to recognize is that, if we are functioning effectively at optimal levels in terms of how well we are able to manage pressures, people and ourselves, then when this proves to be insufficient to address the challenges of the situation, then it is highlighting that there needs to be change in the wider context. That is, by making sure that we are tightening up as far as possible at the micro level, we cast light on any matters that need attention at the macro level.

Motivation is a key factor in this regard, in the sense that the more highly motivated we are, the easier we will find it to manage pressure people and ourselves. It will also be easier to adopt a confident approach to our work if we are highly motivated. Furthermore, it makes it less likely that a culture of low morale will evolve (or continue to apply) if we are motivated. When it comes to self-management, there are at least three important sets of issues that we need to consider.

First, we return to the important concept of values. Values are those things that are important to us, the principles and beliefs that shape our actions and attitudes as well as our feelings and emotional responses. Values are a significant source of motivation and will also sustain us through difficulties. For example, many social workers have told us that they have often considered leaving the profession in search of a less pressurized source of income, and what has stopped them from doing so is their values. They recognize that less pressurized forms of working life are much less likely to satisfy their commitment to making a positive difference to those members of our communities who are most vulnerable and disadvantaged or to promoting social justice. In this regard, values can make all the difference (Moss and Thompson, 2020).

Tiberius (2008, p. 139) argues that: 'cynicism impairs our ability to endorse what we find valuable'. Adopting a defeatist or cynical approach can therefore be seen to both reflect and contribute to our losing sight of our values. Holding on to our values should therefore minimize the risk of descending into defeatism and cynicism, while giving ground to cynicism will make it all the harder to stay connected to our value base.

Second, there is also the significance of professionalism to consider (Parker and Doel, 2013; Thompson, 2016b). As professionals, we can take pride in the knowledge, skills and values that we bring to bear in doing important work. As recognized earlier, despite the negative attentions of the media and the widespread failure of appreciation in terms of the humanitarian endeavours of social work, the work we do is exceptionally valuable in making our society a humane one. In these neoliberal times of managerialism and consumerism, with a defensive emphasis on proceduralization, it can be an easy mistake to make to lose sight of our professionalism. Indeed, we have certainly come across quite a few social work professionals who have become cynical and disengaged and have failed to appreciate the crucial role of professionalism as a basis for ethical and effective practice.

Third, we return to the theme of solidarity. The camaraderie we develop can be immensely important when it comes to motivation and the all-important sense of 'we are in this together'. As noted, though, in times of excessive pressure, there is a tendency for individuals to retreat into their security bubbles and disconnect from others. It is vitally important, if we are to break free from those bubbles and grasp the huge importance of supporting one another as part of a collective endeavour. We need to avoid the vicious circle that produces the ironic situation in which the very time that we need to pull together most is precisely when people are most likely to retreat into their bubble and forego solidarity.

Neither our value base, professionalism nor solidarity is a magic answer. However, each in its own way can make an important contribution and, in combination they can be a very powerful antidote to low morale and the dangers of sliding into negativity, defeatism and cynicism.

Self-leadership

Just as management and leadership are separate but connected entities, so too are self-management and self-leadership. Just as those in leadership positions are called upon to have a clear sense of direction and to shape the culture in ways that support moving people in a positive direction, individuals can draw on self-leadership skills to develop a sense of direction for their own professionalism and broader career, shaping a positive mindset as part of this (mindset being the equivalent for an individual of a culture for a group of people).

We shall return to the subject of having a sense of direction in Chapter 8 when we explore the idea of career planning as a feature of going from surviving to thriving. For now, though, we want to make links between self-leadership and spirituality. We made the point earlier that we should not equate spirituality with religion, as if to suggest that spirituality does not apply to non-religious people. Spirituality is built on finding meaning in our lives, a key part of which is having a sense of purpose and direction, a sense of knowing where we are going with our life (hence the connection with the notion of career).

Self-leadership as a spiritual matter also includes identity and connectedness. Our identity is our sense of who we are and how we fit into the world. Part of this is whether we see ourselves as valued professionals doing a socially very important job (despite what the tabloid press may think), or as passive bureaucrats simply following procedures within an overloaded system.

The spiritual notion of connectedness also brings us back to professionalism. Do we feel that sense of connection with fellow social work professionals, nationally and globally, or is 'social worker' just a job title for some sort of technical role within a faceless bureaucracy?

Connectedness also brings us back to the idea of solidarity and the importance of developing and sustaining a sense of 'we are in this together', as this will strengthen our resolve, give us a much stronger bargaining position when needed, boost our morale and help us to feel safer.

In a sense, self-leadership is the opposite of self-disempowerment. It is about having clarity about who we are, what we want, what our values are, how we are intending to live by them, who and what is important to us and so on. Burnout, organizational toxicity and unrealistic pressures and expectations can lead us into a form of spiritual diminishment that becomes self-perpetuating (in other words, part of yet another vicious circle).

Self-leadership underpins self-management in the sense that it can help us to:

- Keep our pressures in proportion and within manageable limits;
- Have greater confidence in our dealings with other people;
- Be better prepared for managing change and identifying ways of adapting to it and benefiting from it; and
- Have a greater degree of self-efficacy to make us more productive, more in control and therefore better placed to deal with the challenges we face.

Efforts devoted to better understanding self-leadership and developing our capacity for it should therefore be a wise investment of time and energy.

Conclusion

It is to be hoped that this chapter has established the significant role of self-management as an important step on the way to not only surviving, but also thriving. It is part of the wider picture of the various steps that need to be taken and should not be seen in isolation, otherwise it returns us to victim blaming and a failure to balance micro and macro factors.

You may have noticed that one self-management skill (or set of skills) that we have not considered here is that of self-care. This is because the question of self-care (and the associated concept of self-compassion) will feature in Chapter 9 where we shall be focusing on what has come to be known as work-life balance.

In Chapter 10, we shall focus on the various steps that play a part in moving us forward; self-management will be part of this. We shall also be returning to the idea of self-leadership. We will build on some of the important points raised here and, indeed, important issues about self-management will reappear in further elements of the discussion.

We trust that this relatively brief overview of the significance of self-management will be sufficient to encourage you to think carefully about your own self-management and how the insights gained can be of benefit to you in developing them.

Chapter 6: Ensuring Good Practice

Introduction

In this chapter we explore what we regard as some of the key issues as they relate to trying to ensure that we maintain high standards of professional practice even in such difficult and demanding circumstances. The danger, as we see it, is that yet another vicious circle can develop if we are not careful. The weight of pressure upon us can lead us to lower our standards of work, whether by deliberately cutting corners or simply by the overall effect of having so much on our minds. The lower quality of work can adversely affect our confidence and our motivation and therefore add to our pressures while reducing our ability to deal with them.

Being aware of such a vicious circle and its detrimental effects will not automatically deal with the problem, but it is an essential first step. Sadly, some people get drawn into this sort of vicious circle and go on to a sort of automatic pilot without being fully aware that they are doing so. Of course, this is highly dangerous for them, for the people they serve, for the organization they represent and for our profession and its credibility.

So, how do we maintain good or even best practice in the face of such a high level of pressure? There is no simple, formula response to this, but once again there are steps we can take to address the situation. Some of the main ones are precisely what we are going to be exploring here.

Doing the best we can

In his *Lessons for Living* book, Neil makes the point that failure is not simply the opposite of success – it is part of success (Thompson, 2019c). No significant success ever happens without some element of failure preceding it, so it is more helpful to recognize failure as part of success, not as an absence of success. This is not a matter of playing with words – it is a crucial point. We say this because we have come across so many people in social work who become disheartened because they cannot help everyone, they cannot solve all the problems or meet all the needs. We have had to explain to generation after generation of social work students that you cannot expect a 100% success rate. If we do, we will feel guilty about not achieving it and start to see ourselves as failures, rather than people who did the best they could in difficult circumstances.

Imagine how stressful it would be for police officers if they were expected to solve every crime and convict every perpetrator or they convinced themselves that they were somehow a failure in their profession if they did not get everything right. So, we need to be clear that there will be times where we have to get used to there being people we cannot help, needs we cannot meet and so on. This can be very difficult to begin with. Coming face to face with someone who is suffering and not being able to alleviate that suffering is not easy, but it will be the reality of the situation at times. For example, a point that is generally made in training around loss and grief is that you cannot take the pain away. Professionals working with people who are grieving or dying will generally have a strong urge to try and take the pain away. But, this is both an impossible aim and an unhelpful one. It is impossible because the pain is part of the healing. Grieving is a painful, exhausting and frightening experience, but it is a positive one, in so far as it represents the process of readjusting after a major change to our life has occurred. It is unhelpful, because it amounts to failing to honour the loss and can signal to the grieving person that we do not understand what they are going through.

This is what we mean by 'doing the best we can in difficult circumstances'. We are social workers, not miracle workers and there will be much we cannot do, no matter how much we want to. In some ways we are powerful people as social workers, but there will also be many instances where we will be – and feel – powerless. Just as we have to be careful in how we handle our power, we need to be quite circumspect in how we handle our powerlessness.

Disappointment is a function of expectation. What that means is that the more we expect, the more we run the risk of being disappointed. So, if our expectations (of a 100% success rate or close to it) are unrealistic, we are setting ourselves up for unnecessary pressure (and potential distress). What we need to aim for, then, is a balance. Negativity and defeatism are destructive and unhelpful, but so too are unrealistic expectations. We need to find that middle ground of *realism* – being neither unduly pessimistic nor overly optimistic. As professional problem solvers, we should find that sort of realism a major strength. It should enable us to achieve that all-important aim of doing the best we can in difficult circumstances, rather than allowing negativity or unrealistic expectations to make a bad situation worse. This realism can be a good source of personal motivation and can also make a positive contribution to team morale. There is therefore much to be gained from finding that important balance.

Think global, act local

It is perfectly understandable that having to face high levels of pressure day in day out can make us narrow our focus to just concentrating on getting through the day. This means that we lose sight of the bigger picture and, no matter how understandable that may be, it is none the less highly problematic and even dangerous. This is because such a narrow focus on just getting the job done disconnects us from our professional:

- *Knowledge base* We are fortunate in social work to have a huge knowledge base to draw upon to help us make sense of the complexities that are woven into the situations we are trying to influence. For example, working with someone who has been traumatized can be highly challenging work, but the growing theory base around trauma-informed care can be very helpful in deciding how best to respond. Someone whose approach to their work is characterized by the idea of 'head down, get on with it' is unlikely to be able to benefit from that knowledge base, or even to be aware of it. Not making good use of the knowledge base available to us will make us not only less effective, but also more open to criticism.

- *Skills* Good practice in social work relies on a range of important skills. Some of these are extensions of everyday skills, basic abilities taken to a more advanced professional level (communication skills, for example), while others are more specialist, assessment skills being a prime example. The more skilful we are, the more effective we can be and consequently the less pressurized we will be. Skill development can be understood to apply in two main ways: (i) taking existing skills to a more advanced level; and (ii) developing new skills from scratch. We are therefore constantly being presented with opportunities to increase our skill capacity in both these ways. Just 'getting on with the job' is therefore likely to lead to a high proportion of these opportunities being missed. Stagnating is likely to make us less well equipped to cope with our pressure, while continuous skill development is likely to have the opposite effect.

- *Values* We have already made the point that values are important in motivating us and sustaining us through difficult times. They remind us of why the work we do is important and what impact it can have in supporting, protecting and empowering the most vulnerable and disadvantaged members of our communities, If we lose sight of our values, we lose sight of our sense of purpose. If that happens, we face huge pressures but little or nothing to help us withstand them, nothing to remind us that, however difficult the job gets, it is worth doing because of the humanitarian nature of what we do. We should also not forget that values are part of our ethics; they help to 'keep us honest' by making sure that our practice is ethical – that is, fair and humane. Staying in tune with our values is therefore essential not only for our professional integrity, but also our personal integrity as decent human beings.

- *Development* By making sure we continue to learn and develop, we make ourselves more effective, more confident and therefore in a stronger position to manage the relentless pressures we face. Unfortunately, though, a high level of pressure will often serve as a barrier to learning. Focusing narrowly on the tasks in hand will generally deny us the opportunity to learn from our experience. Thompson and Thompson (2018) make the important point that a common misunderstanding of reflective practice is that being busy is a valid reason for not being reflective. The reality, they point out, is that the busier you are, the more reflective you need to be. In other words, the more pressure you are under, the more you need to focus, concentrate and draw on your professional knowledge, skills and values. Switching off and going on to automatic pilot is potentially a recipe for disaster, but sadly a common reaction to high levels of pressure.

- *Identity and pride* The work we do in social work makes a vitally important contribution to making our society a humane and civilized society. We therefore have much to be proud of – especially when you consider the very difficult circumstances in which we carry out our duties. We are also part of a global community or 'family' of social workers who share a commitment to compassion and social justice. If we lose sight of these important elements of

114

our professional role, we lose a significant source of motivation, morale and pride. The fact that certain elements of the media see fit to distort and demonize the work we do does not alter the fact that our society would be much the worse without what we contribute on a regular and consistent basis.

These 'disconnections' are also likely to have an adverse effect on our confidence. The more distant we are from these nurturing and empowering sources, the more of a challenge we face and the less well equipped we will be to rise to it. They also make it more difficult to give and receive support, a point we shall return to in Chapter 7.

What we mean, then, by think global, act local is that we must not lose sight of the big picture. This means: (i) taking account of the macro as well as the micro, as we discussed in Chapter 3; and (ii) keeping in mind how what social workers do on a day-to-day basis makes an important contribution to social welfare.

Both of these implications are important because they have consequences for motivation and morale. If we lose our sense of purpose and value, we run the risk of experiencing a form of spiritual diminishment, a significant impoverishment of our lives. We mentioned earlier (and will mention again later) the importance of the spiritual dimension, not necessarily in religious terms, but in terms of the challenges of meaning, purpose and direction that we face and our sense of 'connectedness'.

Making the most of teamwork

In Chapter 7 we will be examining in some detail the major role that support plays in relation to both surviving and thriving. A key part of that is teamwork. It is also a key part of maintaining good practice, which is why we are also discussing it in this chapter.

One of the things that makes the team so important is that it can be a major advantage or a major disadvantage. That is, where a team works well, the boost it can give members is of major proportions. People can feel empowered, more confident, more positive and safer. A sense of 'we are in this together' can be of immense value and make a huge positive difference. However, where a team does not work well, the opposite can be the case. Poor or non-existent teamwork and the low morale it generates can demotivate people, create unnecessary tensions, make people feel unsupported and unsafe, generate negativity and even defeatism and cynicism. The disempowering effects of a lack of positive teamwork are therefore extremely costly in human terms.

A common misunderstanding is that it is the sole responsibility of the team manager (or equivalent) to make sure that the team functions appropriately. Of course, they do have a prime responsibility, but they can't make it work without the cooperation and commitment of the team members. So, what this means is that everyone has a part to play in trying to make sure that the team environment is a positive, nurturing and empowering one, not a negative, distressing and disempowering one.

This involves being prepared to support one another, to identify tensions and conflicts constructively and respectfully, rather than sweep them under the carpet and/or allow them to eat away at team morale.

What can help is making sure that no one loses sight of the team's purpose. What is it that you are trying to achieve collectively as a team? In other words, what are the team's aims and what are your strategies for achieving those aims? Are these issues clear to everyone in the team? If not, then it very much sounds like you have some teambuilding work to do.

Once again, a vicious circle can arise. A busy team that is not functioning well can fail to move forward positively because the assumption within the team is that 'we are just too busy getting on with the job to get the team issues sorted'. Of course, this is false logic because time taken to resolve those difficulties will be handsomely repaid several times over if addressing the team issues switches the team from being a source of problems and pressure to a source of support and sustenance.

Reaffirming professionalism

Social work in the UK has a rather chequered history in terms of professionalism, going through various phases. We are currently in a phase of reaffirming professionalism in no small part due to the consumerist tendencies associated with neoliberalism that have the effect of reducing social work to largely an administrative process of rationing scarce resources (Parker and Doel, 2013; Thompson, 2016b). These tendencies can add to the pressures while, at the same time, eating away at confidence, morale and professional pride. The reaffirmation of professionalism is therefore an important part of both surviving and thriving. It involves reminding ourselves (and anyone else who will listen) of the value, complexity and significance of what social work achieves in humanitarian terms.

In social work we have a significant professional knowledge base, a wide and varied skills base and an important set of values. We also have a keen awareness of professional accountability as a legitimate expectation of our practice (as opposed to the 'blame culture' of neoliberalism). We are also seeing a growth in our sense of identity, with the British Association of Social Workers going from strength to strength, not only in terms of membership figures, but also in relation to achievements. Added to this, we now have a flourishing union that specializes in promoting the interests – and protecting the rights – of social workers. The Social Workers Union continues to expand in membership and to offer much-needed support and advocacy in these troubled times.

Another aspect of professionalism that can help us both survive and thrive is professional development. Unfortunately, in many quarters, both within social work and beyond, the full significance of continuous professional development (or CPD) has not been realized. To far too many people CPD simply means doing enough training to be able to stay registered. It is what we would call an instrumental approach to professional development. It largely misses the point of what CPD is – or should be – about.

The derivation of the word 'professional' is significant in this regard. It comes from the same root as 'professor' – that is, someone who professes wisdom. Therefore, at the heart of professionalism is a significant knowledge base (hence the emphasis on theory) and the associated wisdom of knowing how to make use of it in practice (hence the emphasis on critically reflective practice).

There is a lot of emphasis these days on 'the knowledge economy' that has grown up to counterbalance the decline in manufacturing. In a very real sense, social workers are knowledge workers. A big part of what makes us effective is the depth and breadth of knowledge and understanding that we can draw upon in terms of people, their problems and needs, the potential ways of addressing them and the potential for growth and flourishing in a spirit of partnership and empowerment – all underpinned by well-developed skills, a solid value base and a commitment to critically reflective practice that pulls it all together.

The knowledge base is far bigger than any one person can absorb (even people who have studied social work for decades will still have much to learn) and is constantly growing. Therefore, if we are genuinely to reaffirm professionalism as a basis for surviving and thriving, we need to go far beyond the simplistic idea that CPD is just a process of ticking boxes. We need to embrace the idea that learning is not something we stop and do every now and again and recognize it as something that needs to be fully integrated into our practice. We need to move away from an 'episodic' approach to learning (learning is what happens on training courses every now and again) and replace it with an *existential* approach to learning – that is, one that sees learning (or at least the potential for learning) as a fundamental basis of what it means to be human.

In his *The Learning from Practice Manual* (Thompson, 2019d), Neil highlights the importance of not only taking our own ongoing learning seriously, but also playing a part in helping others learn. This can give us greater confidence and sense of purpose, as well as a greater degree of job satisfaction and work enrichment – it therefore has spiritual benefits in terms of helping us find meaning (and thus motivation) in our work. It has often been commented on that, in the nursing profession, there is a well-established expectation that qualified nurses share some degree of responsibility for supporting student nurses and others in their learning and development. Sadly, no such tradition exists in social work and so acting as a practice educator or assessor still tends to be seen as an option for those who wish to take it up, rather than a standard expectation that all qualified staff will play their part in promoting learning and thus standards of practice.

The narrow, instrumental approach to continuous professional development also stands in the way of self-directed learning and can thereby prevent us from gaining the benefits of being in control of our own learning. The traditional approach to workplace learning is to see it as the domain of specialists – training managers, staff development officers, workforce development personnel, tutors and so on. These tend to be the people who make decisions about what needs to be learned and by what means (training courses being the most popular option for most organizations).

This approach can have many benefits, not least the build up of expertise, experience and skills in learning and teaching methods. However, one of the drawbacks is that it can – unintentionally – encourage a passive approach to learning on the part of staff and managers. A common scenario is where learners 'get on with the job' and sit back waiting for the 'training people' to make the necessary provision for learning to happen (which usually means organizing and facilitating training courses).

The passivity this promotes can then act as a barrier to learning. For example, we know from our many years of helping people learn that it is very common for people to attend training courses, complete a very positive evaluation form and then return to work as if nothing has happened, with no real integration of the insights gained from the course with actual practice.

Consequently, in terms of reaffirming professionalism – and especially professional development – as part of our drive towards surviving and thriving, there are some cultural changes that we need to work towards, not least the following:

- *Transfer of learning* It is commonly the case that significant sums of money are invested in training provision (which is only one small part of the process of learning), but relatively little in terms of how the work done on courses can be translated into direct improvements in practice. For example, a common complaint from social workers is that their supervision does not include discussion of learning and development – it is reduced to a process of case management or what is often called 'snoopervision' (Thompson and Gilbert, 2019). In addition, it is only a small proportion of organizations that will have some sort of follow-up procedure (for example, a questionnaire a month after the event to ask how the insights gained have been used in practice or, if not, why not). Much depends on whether the organization has a culture of learning that seeks to embed professional development in everyday practice or adopts the 'episodic' approach of seeing learning as something done occasionally as a separate activity from everyday work.

- *Diversity of learning* We have already mentioned that training events tend to be the most popular means of promoting learning. When done properly (and properly followed up), training courses can be excellent sources of learning. However, they are not the only valuable source of learning. If we want learning and development to be genuinely integrated into the day-to-day work of the organization, then we need to move beyond the idea that learning is limited to training. Other options to consider include reflective supervision; guided reading; peer mentoring; involvement in projects; e-learning courses; participation in online learning communities; participation in BASW and/or SWU activities; shadowing a colleague; TED talks; webinars; reflective logs; student supervision; and, perhaps most importantly of all, reviewing our practice and drawing out the lessons to be learned.

- *Self-directed learning* There is a very strong case to be made for self-directed learning being the most effective form of learning because it addresses your own specific learning needs in the ways that work best for you. What we mean by self-directed learning is when you decide for yourself (with appropriate support, as required) what it is you need to learn and choose from the various options in terms of how best you can meet your learning needs (and, again, not restricting yourself to training courses). Self-directed learning is based on the principle that, if you take ownership of your learning, then: (i) time invested in your development can be more accurately targeted to your own specific needs (and not just the general needs of a group of people on a training course, for example); (ii) you are more likely to make sure that the learning actually happens (an active approach, rather than a passive one); and (iii) the learning is likely to be more meaningful to you if it directly addresses the issues you are currently wrestling with. See Thompson (2019d) for more information about self-directed learning.

Professional development can enrich our lives and give us greater strength to manage our pressures and rise to our challenges. It forms an important part of the wider process of reaffirming professionalism and consolidating the value of our work to enable us to be better equipped to not only survive, but also to actually aim for thriving.

Self-care and resilience

We emphasized in Chapter 5 the importance of self-management and in Chapter 9 we shall explore work-life balance. Self-care can be seen to be linked to both of these. Here we want to focus on this topic to make the point that these issues are fundamental to achieving good practice. Realistically, we cannot expect to achieve good practice – let alone best practice – if we are neglecting our own needs. As the saying goes, you can't pour from an empty cup. So, when you reach Chapter 9, it will be very wise to think carefully about how you are going to make sure that you avoid situations where your ability to support others is being undermined by your neglect of your own self-care needs.

This also applies to our direct practice, in the sense that it is not uncommon to find ourselves in a situation where we need to encourage others to think in terms of self-care. An example would be the parents of a severely disabled child who are so devoted to being effective carers that they do not give themselves any downtime and thereby put themselves at risk in terms of stress and potential harm to their physical and mental health. Another example would be someone who looks after an older or disabled person while neglecting their self-care. The net result in both cases is that a vulnerable person can be left unsupported because the person(s) who would normally provide that support have become unavailable. Consequently, this issue of self-care is important for more than one reason.

Resilience, can be understood as 'bouncebackability' – getting back up after adversity has knocked us down. Ideally, we should get back up stronger, having learned from the experience. As with self-care, this applies not only as a personal survival measure, but also as a practice tool. This conception of resilience chimes well with some aspects of social work theory in terms of such matters as:

- *Crisis intervention* Recognizing a crisis as a turning point in a person's life where there is the potential to learn, develop and be empowered by the experience (Thompson, 2018d).

- *Post-traumatic growth* This refers to the opportunities traumatic experiences offer for the people involved to grow and be strengthened as a result of the lessons to be learned, parallel with crisis intervention (Calhoun and Tedeschi, 2006).

- *Transformational grief* An appreciation that, while grieving is a very challenging experience, it offers the potential to come out of the process strengthened by it and better placed to cope with any future losses (Schneider, 2012).

Promoting resilience in ourselves and in others is therefore a worthwhile aim to pursue for both self-preservation and effective practice purposes.

Resilience is one of the Three Rs (Thompson, 2016b) and so it is worth considering how it fits with the other two.

The three Rs

Clearly, resilience is an important concept that we need to be aware of, but it can be helpful to see it as part of a trio of Rs alongside resourcefulness and robustness. It is worth considering each of these in a little more detail.

Resourcefulness

Social work cannot be done effectively by just following guidelines or procedures. While such guidelines and procedures can provide us with a map of the territory, they do not provide an itinerary. That is, we still need to make decisions about what we do: how we make sense of the situations we find ourselves in and how we respond to them. Doing this successfully means that we need to think carefully about what we are doing (another reason for taking reflective practice so seriously) and exploring options. That is where the need to be resourceful comes in. We need to have some degree of creativity in terms of coming up with potential solutions to the problems people are experiencing, imaginative ways of meeting needs, rather than just getting stuck in the tramlines of standardized ways of working. Think of this from your own point of view. If you needed help from a social worker, how happy would you be if they came along and simply tried to slot you into some sort of set pattern, as if they are doing 'painting by numbers', just filling in the blanks, as it were? Would you not be happier if they were using the 'artistry' of which Schön (1983) wrote, the ability to be resourceful in terms of finding helpful ways forward?

Robustness

If resilience is the ability to bounce back after adversity has knocked us down, robustness is the ability to withstand being knocked down in the first place. Indeed, a key part of what resilience is all about is learning from adverse experiences so that we are better equipped to withstand, and deal with, such adversity next time we are challenged by it (as reflected in Nietzsche's well-known idea that 'what does not kill us makes us stronger' – or at least has the potential to make us stronger).

This is not about being tough or macho – it is about being able to learn from the difficult lessons life presents us with so that we are in a stronger position to manage our pressures, keep stress at bay, have greater self-efficacy and a higher level of well-being.

All three of these Rs are therefore very important, but please note that, while we have presented them separately here in order to explain them, they are, in fact, interconnected. Being resourceful enables us to be more robust and more resilient. Being resilient helps us to be more resourceful and more robust, and so on. Promoting the three Rs can be helpful at two levels; first, in terms of our own surviving and thriving and, second, in our practice by recognizing people's strengths in these areas and building on them or building up such strengths where they are needed.

Reaffirming our vision

We very much hope that you came into social work because you had a vision of being able to help, support, protect and empower people, especially the most vulnerable and disadvantaged members of our communities. But, we are very aware that high levels of pressure – especially levels of pressure that are *too* high –

can lead to people losing their vision. We get bogged down in the detail and narrow our focus to just getting through. When that happens, we lose our lifeline. Our vision and the values on which it is based are so important when it comes to surviving – they will often be the difference between going forward and going under. They are also key to thriving, to making sure that we flourish rather than flounder.

Of course, if we recall our discussion in Chapter 5 of spirituality as part of religion, but not restricted to it, we can see these as spiritual matters in terms of our lives (and especially our working lives) needing to have a sense of meaning, purpose and direction as well as a sense of belonging (or 'connectedness', to use the technical term). Revisiting and reaffirming our vision of social work and our part within it are therefore important parts of meeting our spiritual needs. Indeed, our experience of supporting people experiencing stress and/or burnout has highlighted that such problems are in many ways problems of spiritual diminishment. Our work should play a positive role in giving us a sense of fulfilment, but the problems we have been highlighting at various points in this book can be understood as actually denying us such fulfilment, of leaving us with a sense of spiritual impoverishment. Making sure that we do not lose sight of our vision and constantly reaffirm it (for ourselves and for our colleagues) is therefore a key part of both surviving and thriving.

Conclusion

The importance of social work is often not recognized by large sections of the general public, while also prone to vilification at the hands of the low-quality press, but that does not alter the fact that what social workers do on a daily basis is very important indeed in terms of making our society humane, compassionate and fair. We therefore owe it to ourselves, the people we serve, our employers, our profession and, indeed, to society itself to do the best we can in terms of effective practice, despite the immense difficulties we face.

We are certainly fully aware of how significant those difficulties are for the combination of reasons we have been highlighting. We are also aware that these difficulties make it much harder to achieve good practice, but they do not make it impossible. We are back to the key idea of 'doing the best we can in difficult circumstances'. Even if we cannot meet everybody's needs all of the time, we can still endeavour to get the best results possible in straitened circumstances – and we can still feel proud of the important work we do.

Frustration and even anger about how the wider circumstances are combining to create such major difficulties not only for practitioners and managers, but also, very importantly, for the people we serve are quite understandable – are very much to be expected. However, the challenge we face is to try and make sure that these huge difficulties do not prevent us from achieving the best practice possible at the time.

It is to be hoped that the discussions in this chapter will have given you some important insights as well as offered some degree of hope. We offer no simple answers because that would fail to do justice to the complexities involved. However, if you are able to bear in mind the issues we have discussed here, you will be much better placed to make sure that you are able to achieve good practice (surviving) and work towards best practice (thriving).

In a nutshell, our view is that what is needed to ensure good practice is:

- Do the best you can in difficult circumstances: don't expect perfection and don't allow yourself to become a victim of defeatism and cynicism.

- Think global, act local: remember the macro while you wrestle with the micro.

- Make the most of teamwork: good team functioning can make a huge positive difference, so make sure you do the best you can to capitalize on teamwork and encourage others to do so.

- Reaffirm professionalism: don't allow the weight of bureaucracy to lead to the false conclusion that we are not professionals – all professionals have to wrestle with bureaucracy up to a point, but that does not stop them being professionals.

- Take self-care and resilience seriously: don't neglect your own needs. It is not selfish to put your own needs first; in fact, it is a very wise and necessary survival mechanism.

- Remember the Three Rs: try to be as resourceful and robust as you can and these will strengthen your resilience.

- Reaffirm the vision: don't lose sight of the importance and value of social work and the significant part you play in making a positive difference.

Imagine what society would be like if we had no social work. Think that through carefully and you will soon see why we are emphasizing the importance and value of social work and thus the key role you play in 'humanizing' our society.

The obstacles to achieving everything we would like to are at times mountainous and the pressures we face are immense. But, the key message we want to put forward here is that this does not mean that good practice is not possible. We need to hold on to the recognition that our practice, however constrained by wider social and political forces, can still make a difference.

Chapter 7: Using Support

Introduction

We hope that we have made it clear by now that support is an essential part of the equation. Anyone who adopts a macho 'I don't need support' approach is taking a large and unnecessary risk and is also being quite naïve. The uncertainty of life is such that we can encounter situations that challenge our ability to cope at any time in any walk of life. But, in social work, the reality is that challenging situations – sometimes *extremely* challenging situations – are part of the very fabric of what we do. Consequently, we need to be fully tuned in to the different types of support and how these can help. We also need to appreciate some of the main obstacles to using support, including especially our potential unwillingness to ask for it. This is what this chapter is all about, but we begin by clarifying and reaffirming why support is so important.

The importance of support

When we presented the three-dimensional model of stress earlier, we highlighted the positive role of support. The presence of helpful support can both reduce pressures and improve coping (two positives), while the absence of support can increase our pressures and decrease our coping abilities (two negatives). That is, support is crucial in determining whether or not our pressures push us over that all-important line into stress.

It also helps us move away from the oversimplified pathologizing approach to stress that implies that, if you are feeling stressed, it is your own fault for not being able to withstand the pressures. As we have noted, that is a recipe for a vicious circle, and a very destructive one at that. Effective support can, instead, create a virtuous circle – that is, a situation where one positive contributes to another positive and so on, allowing you to go from strength to strength. So, what should happen is that having support makes you feel more confident in tackling your problems and the associated pressures. This will make you better equipped to manage those pressures and this success will then help you feel more confident. Feeling more confident will help you cope better, and so on. And it all begins with support.

However, as we shall see below, there are some added complications we need to take account of if we are to avoid oversimplifying a complex set of issues. First, we need to be aware that there are different types of support and offering the wrong sort at the wrong time can be very unhelpful. For example, if someone is distressed, offering them problem-solving support when all they want or need is for someone to listen to them can be counterproductive, adding a degree of anger and frustration to their distress. Similarly, someone being given advice when what they need is practical, hands-on support can do more harm than good and sour relationships at an important time.

Second, there are various obstacles to support that can get in the way of it being used effectively or used at all. The fact that support exists does not necessarily mean that it will be used. For example, we have come across situations where organizations had supportive measures in place, but most employees did not know about them. We shall explore below some of the main such obstacles and offer some suggestions for how to remove or bypass them or at least minimize their impact.

Support, then, is clearly a key issue, hence our devoting a whole chapter to it. We need to recognize right from the start that support is a general term and can be used quite vaguely at time. We therefore think it is important to be clear about what we mean by it. Consequently, we shall explore in some detail the different types of support and emphasize the need for clarity in terms of what specific type of support is called for. Saying that someone needs support is a good start, but it is not enough on its own. We then need to specify which type of support, why it is needed (with what outcome in mind) and how best to provide it.

Before we look at these different types of support, though, we want to emphasize that the team can be crucial in terms of support, and so we begin by revisiting this important theme of teamwork.

Teamwork revisited

Teams can be a source of considerable support, but they also have the potential to bring about major problems and significantly increased pressures. In view of this, much of what we discuss here will be about how to maximize the positives and minimize the negatives. First, though, we need to be clear what we mean by teams.

Making sense of teams

The notion of team is one that people are generally very familiar with, although it is used in different senses in different contexts which can cause confusion at times. So, to be clear, we are using it here to refer to people united by a common purpose and associated set of goals. Such teams have traditionally shared a physical space within an office, but with the increasing emphasis on 'agile working' and the Covid-19 pandemic-initiated switch towards more home-based working, this can no longer be taken for granted. But, perhaps more importantly, a team will be expected to share some degree of emotional space, in the sense that teamwork involves an emotional commitment ('cathexis', to use the technical term). That is, teams are not just administrative categories; they are psychologically significant sets of social connections and interconnections. How that emotional space is handled will be a key factor in terms of how people manage their pressures and avoid stress, in the sense that teams can either add pressures or help to relieve them.

The social connections and interconnections issue is particularly important, partly because it brings in aspects of diversity to consider and partly because being a member of one or more teams contributes to our social life.

Diversity

In terms of diversity, there are (at least) two main issues to consider. First, it would be naïve to imagine that there will be no differences across team members. There will therefore be diverse opinions, approaches, emphases and priorities. Consequently, an important element of effective teamwork is how well differences and any associated conflicts are managed. Such conflicts can tear teams apart if they are not handled well. Problems can arise when conflicts are allowed to escalate – that is, the tensions enter into a vicious circle that can be very destructive, especially if the conflict leads to people adopting entrenched positions and thereby generating an 'us-them' culture that has the effect of blocking cooperation within the team and creating unnecessary tensions and ill feeling. What can be particularly problematic is when the conflict 'goes underground', in the sense that everybody knows it is there, but nobody talks about it, acknowledges it or does anything about it – but it still manages to undermine morale and significantly reduce the benefits of teamwork.

However, when well managed, conflict can be positive, in the sense that it can bring fresh insights, question taken-for-granted assumptions and challenge complacency. The success of a marriage or equivalent relationship depends not on it being conflict free, but on how well any inevitable conflicts are handled by the couple. The same applies to a team. A conflict-free scenario is unrealistic, but a team where conflicts are handled skilfully, positively and effectively will be in a strong position to make sure that diverse opinions and approaches are not a source of disunity.

Second, another aspect of being a supportive team is, of course, the *valuing* of diversity and inclusion. Recruitment practices that are based on 'cloning' (a 'we appoint "people like us"' approach) result in teams failing to capitalize on the benefits of diversity. The bringing together of different perspectives and approaches serves to enrich a team and this enables it to not only function more effectively, but also to be more supportive.

Similarly, teams that allow discrimination to go unchecked cannot be regarded as functioning effectively, nor as supportive. This whole area is a vast and complex topic that could form the basis of a book in its own right, and so we cannot do justice to it here. What we can do, though, is to note that matters relating to equality, diversity and inclusion have a significant role to play in relation to teamwork, in so far as they can make a highly positive or highly negative contribution, depending on how well they are handled.

Shared responsibility

It is essential to recognize that every member of the team is responsible for making sure that good, supportive teamwork is the order of the day. We mention this because we are aware that many people seem to be under the impression that the manager of the team holds sole responsibility for teamwork. In reality, of course, no manager could be expected to build effective teamwork without the active support and cooperation of the various team members. Promoting mutual support, then, needs to be seen as a shared responsibility across the whole team. Where it is simply assumed that whoever gets paid to lead the team is expected to make sure it happens, but team members themselves have no part to play, the reality of effective teamwork is being oversimplified and distorted to an extent that it makes the team leader's job extremely difficult, if not impossible. The old cliché of 'There's no I in teamwork' reflects the need for team effectiveness (and supportiveness) to be a shared endeavour across all team members.

Humour

One further ingredient of a supportive team is humour. Having fun together can be a major feature of team bonding. A team that laughs together stays together may not be entirely true in all cases, but there is no doubt that the appropriate use of humour can be a positive component of solid teamwork. We say 'appropriate' because humour can sometimes be used cynically and/or cruelly. For example, some degree of 'gallows humour' can be positive and helpful, but, when taken to extremes, can undermine morale and reinforce negativity and defeatism. Perhaps the most supportive thing a team can do is to instil, and do justice to, a sense of solidarity, a sense that 'we are in this together'. Part of this can be making it clear that no stigma is attached to asking for support – support is what the team is all about. Humour can be part of the 'glue' that binds us in that solidarity or a contribution to pushing us apart. How valuable or destructive humour is will therefore depend on the type of humour and how it is used. For example, if it is used to mock people who are struggling or who express a need for support, then it can be catastrophic for teamwork. However, when used wisely and ethically, it can bring people together in a spirit of shared commitment and mutual support.

Obstacles to effective team support

It would be naïve to assume that there will never be obstacles to supportive teamwork. Such barriers can be very significant in preventing the development and maintenance of team support. It is therefore worth exploring some of the main obstacles, on the basis that forewarned is forearmed.

- *Competitiveness* While not necessarily a problem in its own right, competitiveness can become a significant obstacle to teamwork when it stands in the way of cooperation and solidarity. Competitiveness can encourage team members to see one another as opponents, rather than as allies. This can create jealousy and rivalries and these generally tend to be bad news, in the sense that: (i) it encourages a narrow focus on the specifics of whatever is being competed over, rather than more holistically on the team's overall purpose and the outcomes it is intended to achieve; and (ii) a focus on 'winning' can lead some people to abandon their values and engage in unethical behaviour, such is their desire to win out against their 'opponents'. A limited amount of friendly competition within an overall culture of solidarity can be fine, but when a culture of competition develops, this is likely to be at a high price in terms of support and camaraderie.

- *Cliques* It is quite understandable that subgroups will form within larger groups, and this is not necessarily a problem when it arises. However, this situation can prove to be quite harmful when it contributes to an 'us-them' mentality and subtle – or, sometimes not-so-subtle – processes of exclusion. Subgroups that support one another for the overall good of the team (and thus the organization and, importantly, the people it serves) are clearly making a positive contribution. However, when subgroups reach the point where they undermine one another, create unnecessary tensions and stoke conflicts, the term "clique" becomes applicable. This term is the appropriate one, as it implies not simply a set of subgroups, but also a set of destructive dynamics that are likely to put paid to a supportive team or an environment that helps people flourish.

- *Security bubbles* This phenomenon is one we have already referred to. Superficially, it sounds fine that individuals under significant pressures retreat into some sort of safe haven, as they perceive it. However, where this prevents solidarity from developing and acts as a block to a collective response to shared problems, we can begin to see the potential dangers. We all need a degree of security, of course, but a supportive team should be able to provide a degree of *shared* security, so that we do not need to rely on bubbles that have the effect of isolating us (and thereby rendering us more vulnerable).

- *Poor or non-existent leadership* When exploring workplace issues, it usually does not take long before leadership comes to be seen as an issue. Leaders have a duty to shape the culture in a positive direction – including in a supportive direction, of course. Consequently, where there is a failure of leadership, there can be a significantly reduced likelihood of supportive teamwork developing or being sustained over time. We discussed earlier the historic struggle in UK social work to get leadership on the agenda and to provide the necessary training and support to nurture the quality and quantity of leadership that we need. While we are clearly moving in the right direction, we still have much work to do in this regard.

- *Divisive management* In our experience, it is sadly the case that a small proportion of managers can be deliberately divisive as a result of their own feelings of insecurity about team members becoming more powerful than they are if everyone works together. More common, but just as destructive, are managers who are not intending to be divisive, but who lack the self-awareness to realize that this is precisely what their style of management contributes to. For example, there can be an unconscious bias towards certain individuals or certain categories of people – along gender or ethnic lines in many cases. Where people suspect – rightly or wrongly – that there is favouritism or any other sort of unfair bias going on, considerable ill feeling can be generated – something that will no doubt have a seriously detrimental effect on teamwork and, indeed, on team morale.

- *Toxicity* This important concept that we encountered earlier refers to: (i) behaviours, such as bullying and harassment and discrimination and; (ii) aspects of the culture that can do harm (a "blame" culture, for example, where it is falsely assumed that, if something goes wrong, there must be one or more individuals who need to be pilloried and punished for this). Addressing toxicity can bring people together and promote supportiveness, whereas allowing such matters to go unchallenged is likely to lower morale and make the team less supportive. Interestingly, while the term toxicity tends to be used in relation to organizations, it takes little stretch of the imagination to see that the same issues it raises can also apply to some families and communities and therefore be relevant to direct social work practice as well as the challenges we face within our own organizations.

There is no simple formula or magic answer for making teams supportive but, as we have seen here, there are steps that can be taken to promote and sustain team support and barriers to such support that we can challenge and seek to remove or at least minimize. Team support is an important factor for building resilience and stamina in order to withstand pressures. It is therefore worthy of a significant investment of time, effort and thought.

Types of support

We made the point earlier that the terms 'support' can be used very vaguely at times, with little or no precision about what that means. It can therefore be helpful to explore the main different types so that you can consider the various ways in which support can be offered and aim to ensure that we are being as effective as possible in terms of the support we seek to offer one another.

- *Practical support* When people are under a high level of pressure, even the slightest extra task can appear insurmountable at times. Consequently, when someone is offering practical help by, for example, undertaking one or more tasks on our behalf the relief can be immense. As the name implies, practical support is simply the provision of direct support at a very practical level, geared towards taking pressure off people who are under considerable strain (while also giving what can be a vitally important message of: you are not alone; we are in this together). It would include such offers as:

"Here, let me do that for you";
"Sit down and take a break; I'll make you a coffee";
"I'll drop that off for you to save you a trip";

and so on. In some circumstances, straightforward practical support of this kind can make all the difference between coping and not coping, between surviving and going under (for example, through stress-related sickness absence). This takes us back to our theme of vicious circles. Person A needs some practical support, but Person B feels too busy to offer it because of the level of pressure they are under. Person A then becomes stressed and is therefore not able to offer support to Person B when they need it. But, it does not have to be that way. We can create 'virtuous circles' by making sure that we find that extra bit of energy somewhere to offer that little bit of practical support where and when it is needed.

- *Emotional support* Often referred to as moral support, this includes being prepared to listen non-judgementally, talking sensitive issues through and validating or affirming feelings. For example, in our work in relation to death, grief and bereavement or other major losses, emotional support very often boils down to "being there" for someone. Words of reassurance or solace also have a significant role to play in this regard. Sadly, when people get too busy, the result can be that offering reassurance is neglected – people rush on to the next task on their list and miss the opportunity to make an important contribution to being supportive. What is particularly significant about this is that a failure to offer reassurance or solace when they are needed can not only fail to provide support, but also create ill feeling, disappointment and resentment if it is perceived as expressing a lack of concern, interest or care. In this respect, our efforts to be supportive can be counterproductive. This applies in relation to both our direct practice and with our efforts to support one another through difficult circumstances. Any neglect of emotional support therefore comes at a high price. As with practical support, a crucial component of this is giving people the message that there is someone who cares about them, someone who is prepared to help and thereby reinforce the all-important message that 'we are in this together'.

- *Resource-based support* This involves providing or facilitating access to resources of whatever kind are needed. What those resources might be will vary from setting to setting, circumstance to circumstance, but again that crucial message of "we are in this together" can be just as important as the resource provided. We are aware that frustration around access to resources is a common challenge for social workers, and so the more tuned in we are to resource-based support, the better.

- *Confidence-boosting support* People who are stressed or at risk of stress because of high levels of pressure can easily lose confidence and start to doubt themselves, potentially setting up a vicious circle whereby the lower level of confidence acts as a barrier to managing their pressures effectively. In some cases, 'impostor syndrome' can be experienced. This refers to confidence reaching such a low level that the person concerned feels like an impostor, as if they do not deserve to be in the role they occupy, that they are not worthy of their job. It is not uncommon in situations where levels of pressure lead to even highly competent people experiencing considerable struggles to get their work done. It is a dangerous phenomenon, and it will no doubt come as no surprise to hear us say that there is a danger here of one or more vicious circles developing. Taking sensitive steps to help boost confidence can therefore prove to be highly beneficial. We say "sensitive" steps because, if not done tactfully, such efforts can come across as patronizing. Fear of getting it wrong, though, should not hold us back from engaging in confidence-boosting support, as it can make such a positive difference, while its absence can add extra pressures and contribute to destructive processes of self-disempowerment holding sway.

- *Problem-solving support* We mentioned earlier the problem of people retreating into their "security bubble", rather than supporting one another. Where this occurs, it can mean that people are forced to face problems alone and can easily become overawed or even overwhelmed by them. As social workers, we should be well aware that, when it comes to problem solving, two heads are generally better than one. A second perspective on the situation can help cast new light on aspects of the problem and potential solutions. Someone offering to sit down with you, develop an understanding of the problem and explore possible solutions can therefore be making an extremely supportive move. This is another reason why the retreating into our security bubble strategy is not the wisest way to tackle the problems we face. It can so easily lead to an attitude of 'You focus on your problems and I will focus on mine', rather than the much more effective attitude of: 'I'll help you with your problems and you can help me with mine'. The emotional support that comes as sort of 'bonus' to this can also be invaluable.

- *Employer support* What should be happening, of course, is that senior management teams should be ensuring that employees are receiving appropriate support through supervision, appraisal, training and development, occupational health services and so on and possibly also from an Employee Assistance Programme (offering, for example, confidential counselling). The situation in actual practice will, of course, vary considerably. Some organizations offer excellent support in some areas, but not so good in others. The key point, though, is that it is important to make full use of whatever support is available. Unfortunately, in situations characterized by low morale, it is not uncommon for such support to be underused or even misused – for example:

- o Supervision can become a moaning shop, rather than a valuable process of professional support and development; and/or
- o People do not sign up for training, or sign up but don't turn up, or turn up and simply use it as a break from office demands.

- *Union or professional organization support* Of course, as we are both staunch supporters of trade unionism as a force for good, not only in the workplace, but also in society more broadly, and longstanding supporters of our professional organization, our advocacy of the role of unions and professional organizations should not come as a surprise. There are various types of support available through being a member of a trade union or professional organization, including advocacy and collective bargaining in relation to conditions of employment. We have emphasized repeatedly the key role of solidarity and this is, of course, what trade unions and professional organizations are all about. It is, of course, wise to have the backing of an organization that has our interests at heart and some degree of power and influence to promote and protect those interests, while going it alone has many risks. We are fortunate in the UK to have a well-established professional organization (BASW) and can add trade union membership (SWU) to that for a small additional subscription. Trade unions and professional organizations have an important role to play in ensuring workplace justice at any time, but especially so in the particularly challenging times we face in contemporary social work.

These different types of support will overlap at times, of course, and at times some people will struggle to get access to any of them. It is indeed a complex picture, but all that needs to concern us at present is that we are not reluctant to give, receive or ask for support.

Obstacles to using support

Just as there were obstacles to using teamwork that were worth exploring on the basis that forewarned is forearmed, there are barriers to using support. Our discussion of the importance of support and the different forms it can take will have been a complete waste of time and energy if we fall victim to one or more of the common obstacles to using support. Our focus, then, in the rest of this chapter is on identifying some of these barriers so that we will be better placed to deal with them in whatever reasonable ways we can when it comes to how to remove or bypass them, or at least minimize their impact.

- *Stigma* As we have noted, the stigma commonly associated with stress can so readily act as a barrier to asking for support. This is why it is so very important to challenge such stigma and move away from narrow, individualistic approaches to pressure and stress that pay little or no attention to the very important macro-level factors. As social workers schooled in anti-discriminatory practice, we should be well aware of the harmful impact of stigma. Applying demeaning or disempowering labels to people is sadly a common and longstanding feature of our society and a regular feature of some aspects of what we encounter in social work (in relation to mental health, for example). The fact that stress, or even the asking for support to prevent stress, has come to be seen as a sign of weakness and therefore stigmatized is a sad reflection of the lack of understanding of what happens when people are exposed to excessive levels of pressure and a lack of empathy in relation to the extreme distress that can be involved. We therefore need to do whatever we can – individually and collectively – to challenge and reduce stigma.

- *A macho culture* Partly as a result of the stigma and partly as a contributory factor to the development of such a harsh attitude, 'macho' cultures are not uncommon, even in the caring professions. Such cultures are characterized by a "be tough" mentality and an "If you can't stand the heat, get out of the kitchen" attitude. The message such a culture gives is: only weak people ask for support, so we will think badly of you if can't consume your own smoke. Clearly, such an approach is highly problematic. In addition to the stigma we have already discussed, a macho culture presents a serious barrier to a compassionate approach to people who, for whatever reason, are struggling to cope with the pressures they face. A macho culture is clearly a problem and so, the sooner it is recognized that a macho culture has no place in social work (and, ideally, in any workplace), the better.

- *Being locked in a vicious circle* We have commented on a number of occasions in earlier chapters on the dangers of vicious circles evolving. By their very nature, they can be very destructive and, in particular, they can serve as an obstacle to support being asked for or offered. Ironically, support is normally precisely what is needed to break such vicious circles. Commonly, part of one particular vicious circle can be the retreat into a security bubble, as discussed earlier, resulting in a narrow self-isolating focus on just getting through the day, rather than getting support, wherever possible, to tackle whatever is making them feel the need to withdraw. Similarly, excessive pressures and unrealistic workload expectations can generate a 'heads down, get on with it mentality' that leads to jumping from one task to the next, with no time taken to consider what is happening or what can be done to address the problems leading to the overload situation. Supporting one another to break out of vicious circles can therefore be understood as an important part of any support strategy.

- *Unresponsive management* Of course, the quality of management in any organization can vary considerably. Like most other vocational or professional groups, some managers are very poor, some are excellent, and most will be somewhere in between. There will, therefore, be times when the quality of management leaves a lot to be desired and this will often manifest itself in the form of unresponsive and unsupportive management on the part of some people. What can also happen is that managers who are normally very good at their job can become unresponsive because they are struggling to cope with their own pressures (and so the potential for another vicious circle arises). What we must not do is overgeneralize and oversimplify by indulging in some sort of 'manager bashing' game. What we are talking about is a minority of managers or certain managers in understandable circumstances. If we are to have a genuinely supportive workplace culture, then we need to leave behind unfair overgeneralized criticisms, while also being aware that unresponsive management can be a problem at times. We would do better if we were to support one another in looking at what is causing such unresponsiveness, rather than risk being involved in what could amount to scapegoating.

Being aware of these various obstacles will, of course, make no difference unless we come up with one or more strategies for tackling them. Each of us can think about how we can address those obstacles that apply directly to us, while also potentially playing a part in a collective endeavour (at the team level, for example) to make your working environment as supportive as possible for you and your colleagues.

Conclusion

The following comment made by a participant on a training course about stress tells a sad story:

> I was a police community support officer before I came into social work. I got plenty of support in the police. But, what really surprised me after making the transition was that I had expected social services to be even more supportive, but that didn't turn out to be the case. People were so busy that everyone was running round trying to get stuff done. Nobody seemed to have time to sit down and support one another. Where I am now is much better, but still not as good as it was in the police.

Of course, the experience of just one individual is not necessarily representative, but it does chime well with our broader experience of supporting people through difficult times. The basic message is this: the fact that social work is one of the caring professions does not guarantee that a great deal of support and caring will be available for staff. The reality, according to our extensive experience, is that there is huge variation across social work organizations, ranging from excellent support to virtually non-existent. But, even in the excellent examples, there will always be scope for improvement, of course.

We hope that the exploration in this chapter of the importance of support, the key role of teamwork, the different types of support and obstacles to support being offered or taken up will be of value in working out what steps can be taken to maximize the quality and quantity of support available and to minimize the likelihood that people will face huge pressures without adequate support.

A key step that everyone can take is to be prepared to ask for support when we need it (and not just when we are starting to get desperate), be prepared to offer it to colleagues whenever we have concerns about them and, where necessary, be part of a process of culture change that challenges the idea that needing support is a sign of weakness.

Chapter 8: Career Planning

Introduction

One of the consequences of working in a context where pressures are excessive is that people will tend to focus on the here and now, just on getting through the week, or even just the day. This means that they will lose sight of the longer-term picture of their overall career path. This can be problematic because having a sense of career, with associated goals to aim for, can be an important source of motivation. As we shall see in more detail in this chapter, it is not simply a matter of naked ambition to get to the top; the situation is actually more complex than that.

A key factor in terms of career planning is getting the balance right between a sense of ambition on the one hand and stagnation on the other. As we shall see, neither of these extremes is helpful or productive and can contribute more to the problems than to the potential solutions. Part of that challenge is getting a balance between the attractions of money, power and status on the one hand and job satisfaction and spiritual fulfilment on the other. Too much of an emphasis on the former can lead to a situation in which your career is managing you, rather than you are managing it (another example of a self-management challenge).

We have already mentioned the importance of self-leadership which involves having a sense of direction. So, when it comes to career planning, an important question to ask is: what journey are you on? Do you have a destination in mind or are you just enjoying the ride and taking in the sights? Interestingly, this reflects the differences in eastern philosophy between the approach of Confucius, who emphasized order, and Buddha, whose teachings warn against investing energy in projects driven by desire that are likely to lead to disappointment.

Whichever approach you take, the carefully planned or the more flexible, the need for a balanced approach remains. In this chapter, we help you to consider your options by exploring first of all what is meant by the concept of career, then examining some key issues relating to options available in terms of career development over time.

What do we mean by career?

We noted earlier that work is an important element of people's lives. As Hamer (2007) comments:

> Work is what we do most of our waking lives. Work is central to our happiness and our feelings of self-worth. We see ourselves reflected in our work, in the outcome and importance of what we do. When we think about our lives we often define ourselves in terms of how we make a living. We spend an awful lot of our life working, trying to make a living and trying to express our individuality. The function of work is to pay for our lives and homes and support our families, and yet employment also gives us the opportunity to express ... our individuality.
>
> (p. 4)

Given the importance of work in our lives, we can see that the notion of career is a significant one. But, what do we actually mean by career?

The conventional approach to the concept of career development tends to be quite simplistic. It is construed as a ladder to be climbed, with the rungs representing a series of potential promotions that are intended to bring greater power, status, income and, in principle at least, respect. However, this conceptualization is problematic in at least two main ways. First, it tends to be based on the assumption that promotion is necessarily a good thing. Second, if fails to take account of what is known as the horizontal career model which involves not necessarily working towards promotion (a vertical model), but rather broadening horizons horizontally in terms of taking on further roles and responsibilities with a view to gaining greater job satisfaction, being in a better position to make a positive difference and finding a working life that is positive for us in terms of our spiritual needs. These are both important points, and so we shall consider each in turn in a little more detail.

However, before we do that, we should acknowledge the significance of career development as a basis for moving from surviving to thriving. If we are going to want to do more than settle for merely surviving and strive for the best results we can possibly achieve despite the very difficult circumstances of modern social work, we need to consider what our career means to us and how we intend to manage it. It is our hope that this chapter will help you begin (or continue) that process.

Linked to this is the importance of professionalism. We have already emphasized that a strong focus on professionalism is a central element of both surviving and thriving. If we see ourselves as simply bureaucrats following procedures, rather than as well-educated professionals committed to humanitarian values, we will struggle to survive without some degree of burnout or disengagement. Similarly, what can lift us and drive us forward as we aim for thriving is a recognition of the value and significance of what we do as social work professionals. Consequently, as we consider issues relating to career development, both now as we work our way through the chapter and beyond this, we need to do so in the context of the importance of professionalism (Parker and Doel, 2013; Thompson, 2016b).

Climbing the ladder

Dominant understandings of the notion of career tend to present it as an ongoing process of upward mobility. Each promotion is understandably seen as something to be proud of and something we should welcome. However, the reality is far more complex. This is because it is not uncommon for people to be promoted and find that the change in their working circumstances may bring some positives, but does not necessarily produce a working life scenario that is an overall improvement on their previous job. Sadly, what is perceived as a loss of face in returning to their previous level of employment means that many people remain in a job that pays better than their previous position, but which brings far less satisfaction and could actually be a significant obstacle to happiness and well-being.

We have come across a minority of people who made the step back and were glad that they did – for example, people who have taken on management positions at a higher salary, only to return to a practitioner post in due course because they found that more satisfying and more suited to their needs, despite the return to a lower salary. However, we have come across a much higher number of people who have confided in us that they miss their previous role, but feel unable to return to such a role, partly because they have become accustomed to the higher standard of living afforded by the higher salary, but often more so by the sense of embarrassment at what could be perceived as a failure.

What is also significant is the culture of materialism we discussed earlier. The potential for earning more money is a powerful driving force for most people. It is a motivation that is strongly reinforced by popular culture and the mass media, particularly by commercial groups who have a vested interest in materialism. It is not without its drawbacks, though. As Pickering (2012) explains:

> Gandhi remarked that 'The world has enough for everyone's needs, but not for some people's greed'. Someone who experiences the world from this viewpoint will feel fundamentally secure. Corporate greed, acquired second- hand via the advertising industry, makes people feel insecure. The world cannot seem ever to provide enough. ... Artificial needs created through media stimulation, by contrast, are designed specifically not to be met.
>
> (p. 161)

Where people's sole motivation to pursue promotion is financial, there is a danger that unwise decisions will be made. People who set their sights on getting to the top and increasing their income at every stage can easily lose sight of other important things in life, not least their professional values.

We need to be very wary of the dangers of allowing materialistic considerations to distract us. We need to make sure that efforts to achieve security and well-being are not channelled exclusively or even primarily through the acquisition of material goods and the competitiveness that such materialism generates.

One consequence of such materialism has been the dumbing down of social life, especially in popular culture (as, for example, in the popularity of 'reality television' programmes). Added to this is the cult of celebrity that fuels so many people's desire to be rich and famous, despite the significant body of evidence to suggest that such ambitions, even if realized, are unlikely to be spiritually fulfilling.

It is to be hoped that social workers are sophisticated enough not to become victims of this kind of populist mindset, but it must be recognized that the influence of such thinking is both pervasive and persuasive, and so it would be complacent not to recognize the dangers involved.

Similarly, many people will be attracted to the vertical career route by the chance to have greater power and status. However, with increased power comes increased responsibility and, in the current circumstances, very many people are finding that extra responsibility quite onerous. We are by no means trying to discourage anyone from applying for promotion. Rather, what we are trying to do is to highlight some important issues that many people fail to consider due to their ambition.

The key point we want to emphasize here, therefore, is this: if you are tempted to climb the ladder, it is worth considering what your main motivation is, and, depending on what your answer should be, whether pursuing promotion is your wisest option.

We therefore need to be wary of uncritically accepting this commonsense conception of career as a ladder to be climbed, with the questionable assumption that this is always or even generally a good thing. We have found that a common motivation for climbing the ladder is not only the obvious matter of salary and status, but also having become bored with their previous job. This is where the idea of a horizontal approach to career planning becomes important.

Horizontal career development

Increasingly, it is being recognized that there is more to career planning than a simplistic notion of promotion after promotion. There is now a growing awareness of the negatives associated with what can become a ruthless ambition to get to the top, an ambition that can lead to losing friends, gaining enemies and having a less satisfying and less fulfilling life. People who focus narrowly on getting to the top (however that is defined) run the risk of missing out on other aspects of life, getting a reputation for being self-serving and failing to get full satisfaction from what they are doing in the here and now, because their focus is constantly on the next rung of the ladder.

149

Basically, what a horizontal career development approach entails is looking for opportunities to extend yourself in terms of your knowledge, skills and values, taking your professional development seriously, not simply as a requirement for registration purposes, but as a way of gaining greater fulfilment.

An important concept to consider here is that of 'existential learning' (Thompson, 2019d). This is the opposite of instrumental learning (which involves simply learning how to get the job done). Instrumental learning has its place (for example, knowing how to use a particular piece of software or knowing which form to fill in according to the particular circumstances), but it is certainly not enough. Existential learning goes far beyond this, in so far as it involves growing and developing as a person (that is, learning that shapes who you are, hence the term 'existential').

Simply learning in an instrumental way will not contribute to horizontal career development in any significant way, whereas existential learning can. This brings us into the spiritual realm in terms of meaning, purpose, direction and our sense of who we are and how we fit into the world. We shall therefore return to this point below when we consider career as a spiritual matter.

In these days of flat hierarchies in organizations, as discussed in Chapter 1, opportunities for advancement in the vertical sense have been significantly curtailed as a result of the wider situation in previous years. This can lead to stagnation for many experienced professionals who feel they are ready for the next step in their career, but have little opportunity in terms of vertical advancement.

Finding one or more means of avoiding such stagnation is precisely what horizontal career development is all about; it can prevent us becoming restless and dissatisfied.

However, it is not simply a matter of coping with the lack of vertical opportunities, it is also, more holistically, about recognizing that, while horizontal career development will not necessarily increase income, it can be more satisfying in a number of ways than the conventional climbing the ladder approach. Horizontal development opportunities would include:

- *Supervising junior staff and/or students on placement* There may be opportunities to supervise junior staff from time to time – for example, support workers or equivalent. This may begin as a joint supervisory arrangement along with their existing supervisor until you have the skills and confidence to undertake the work on a solo basis.

  There may also be a role for you in terms of supporting one or more newly qualified staff to complement wider efforts to help them make the transition from student to fully fledged worker.

  Then, of course, there is also the possibility of contributing to practice learning by supervising students on placement, whether as an onsite supervisor or as a full-scale practice teacher / educator. As anyone who has been involved in this type of work over time will tell you, it can be very rewarding work.

- *Supporting colleagues pursuing in-house qualifications* There may also be opportunities to support people who are involved in some form of qualification that is work based, rather than college based (or a mix of work and college based). This would include staff pursuing vocational qualifications.

  If you are very experienced in the mental health field, there may be scope for you to act as a study supervisor or equivalent for one or more colleagues undertaking Approved Mental Health Practitioner training. As with student supervision, you may be able to do this on a joint basis to begin with until you are ready to work on a solo basis.

  Helping people learn can take up a fair amount of time, but the benefits to be gained can be a significant source of motivation that enables us to get more done in the remaining time. As Thompson (2019d) explains:

  > Promoting learning from practice can be hard work, often with no extra pay or tangible rewards. However, despite this, it can be immensely rewarding, both intrinsically and through the exciting process of engagement with learning itself and from the satisfaction of knowing that you have played a positive part in contributing to high standards of professional practice and to creating and sustaining workplaces based on continuous learning and

development.

(p. 13)

It can be particularly beneficial when the learning promoted is of the existential kind.

- *Mentoring minority group staff* Some organizations have a scheme whereby they offer mentoring support to members of minority groups, whether black or ethnic minority (BAME), LGBTQ+ or any other group where discrimination is likely to be a potential issue. If such a scheme exists in your organization, might you be able to contribute to it in some way? If no such scheme exists, might you be able to work with like-minded colleagues to develop such a mentoring programme?

- *Contributing to policy development, service planning or other such initiatives* There may be times when an employing organization will set up a planning group, whether on an ongoing basis or time limited (what is often called a 'task and finish' group). If such groups exist in your organization, might you be able to make a contribution in some way? If you are not aware of any such groups, who would you need to speak to in order to find out and register your interest?

  You do not have to be an expert in social policy to make a worthwhile contribution, but your knowledge, experience and particular perspective could potentially be of great use.

- *Secondment* Organizations that are highly committed to learning and development will often use secondment as a means of creating learning opportunities. This involves temporarily changing team, department or role in order to broaden and deepen your experience. How this works in many organizations revolves around maternity leave. So, when a woman goes on maternity leave, instead of bringing in a temp to cover her role, someone from another team can be given the opportunity to switch role for the duration of the leave period. The temporary vacancy the switch creates can then either be filled by a temp or used to create a secondary secondment opportunity – that is, someone from a different team fills that slot as their own learning opportunity.

- *Contributing to newsletters within your own organization or seeking publication beyond your organization* If your organization has a newsletter, can you contribute to it in some way? This could be writing articles, providing news and/or photographs, being involved in editing and production and so on. If your organization does not have one, could you be involved in developing one?

  You might also be able to contribute to a newsletter published by your union or professional organization. Getting your name in print can be very satisfying and reinforce your professional identity.

  Similarly, writing for publication can be very rewarding. This could range from an article for a local newspaper through to a prestigious academic journal. Of course, you would have to ensure that confidentiality is not breached. In addition, some employers do not allow their staff to use information gained from within their workplace, even if it is anonymized. It would therefore be wise to check. But, even if no permission is required, it can be wise to inform your employers of any submissions you may make, simply as a matter of professional courtesy.

- *Undertaking further qualifications* One example of this would be attempting to achieve an advanced-level qualification in some aspect of your practice sphere. This could be a generic-type qualification, such as a Master's degree in advanced practice or something more specialist, such as a Master's in family therapy. However, such developments need not be at Master's level. A certificate or diploma in counselling, mediation or other such aspect of practice could also be very worthwhile.

- *Contributing to teaching or training* It is quite common for colleges and universities to rely on practitioners to contribute to some aspects of teaching on social work qualifying courses. Is this something that could help you to develop your horizontal career options? Could you contribute to teaching, even if just in a small way – to begin with at least? Opportunities can range from being a guest speaker alongside a tutor at one extreme to running a whole module on your own at the other.

  Similarly, there may be scope for you to contribute to training within your own organization. This too has a broad range, from, say, a half hour slot as part of a training day where you talk about a specialist area of practice   through to being fully responsible for a training course or programme.

- *Research* Opportunities to be involved in research projects do not come up very often, but where they do, this too can be an important part of horizontal career development. There is also, of course, the potential to undertake your own small-scale research project, especially if you can muster support from one or more people with experience in managing research projects, either within your organization or beyond. Practitioner research can be invaluable, but, unfortunately, we do not have a strong tradition of such research in social work (compared with, say, nursing or medicine). Perhaps you could play a small part in changing that. If you wanted to pursue this, who would be the key people who could support you in your endeavours?

- *Involvement in external projects* On occasion, you may get chance to be involved in a multidisciplinary or multi-agency project of some kind. As Smith and Smith (2008) explain:

  > Another possibility for helpers who feel constrained by the culture, expectations and requirements of their organization is to develop the work in other settings, or in association with other groups or agencies. There are various options here. One is to use umbrella organizations – especially those that the organization is already associated with.
  >
  > (p. 146)

  Such possibilities may not come along very often, but being aware that they might can help you to stay alert to the potential to capitalize on any that do arise from time to time.

- *Trade union or professional organization activities* These can be at formal or informal levels. By formal, we mean standing for office in some way, such as by aiming to serve on a committee of some sort. Being a workplace representative for your union would also be included under this heading. By informal, what we mean is doing whatever you reasonably can to support trade union and professional organization aims. This would include attending meetings and conferences and encouraging colleagues to join.

This is not an exhaustive list of examples of the ways in which you can become a more rounded professional, create more and better opportunities for job satisfaction and fend off the dangers of boredom and stagnation if you have been doing the same job for a long period of time. However, it should put across a clear message that upward mobility is not the only way to achieve career development.

Interestingly, career advancement in a horizontal sense will also, in some cases, mean that you are better placed in terms of potential vertical advancement, if that is what you want to pursue. For example, in applying for promotion, if you are able to demonstrate that you have been involved in some or all of the activities listed above, you are likely to come across as more impressive and a better catch than someone who has not taken the trouble to develop in this way, someone who has just continued to do their day-to-day job without any noticeable contribution to the wider good of the organization and, importantly, the people it serves. Compare, for example, the following two hypothetical promotion applicants:

Person A: Has four years of relevant experience, has performed well and has no significant blemishes in their track record, but has done nothing other than fulfil the basic requirements of the job.

Person B: Also has four years of relevant experience, has performed well and has no significant blemishes in their track record, has supervised students, helped to set up a mentoring scheme for minority group colleagues and has served on a policy review committee.

There will obviously be a range of factors that a selection panel would need to consider before making an appointment, but which of these two candidates is likely to have a head start?

It is to be hoped, then, that this discussion will help you to appreciate that there is more to career planning than people generally realize. Arguably, people who are grossly ambitious to get to the top are often the people who are less well equipped to be effective leaders when they get there, because what has been driving them has been naked self-interest, rather than a commitment to positive results for their colleagues, their organization and the people the organization serves.

Your career path

As we have noted, it is perfectly acceptable for you to take each step in your career as it comes, to not have any grand plan for your own personal advancement, other than wanting to achieve the best results that you are capable of in difficult circumstances. However, if your preference is to map out a career plan, it too is perfectly acceptable, provided that: (i) you do not allow any such ambitions to lead to unethical behaviour (being a 'neck treader', someone who will happily gain an advantage at other people's expense): and (ii) you are sufficiently flexible to adapt your plans as circumstances change. Without an ethical approach you will be potentially a danger to others and, without flexibility, you will be potentially a danger to yourself in terms of creating considerable disappointment and heartache when what you were firmly committed to appears not to be a possibility. Once again, it is a matter of balance.

If you do have the intention of developing in advance a career plan, it is important to explore the potential options available in the short, medium and long terms. It is important to know what such options are before developing a detailed plan, otherwise you may never become aware of something that could actually suit you very well.

What is also very important is the fundamental question of whether or not you are in the wrong job. This may strike you as a strange question to ask, but our experience has taught us that it is not uncommon for people to be struggling in their job because they are in the type of role that is not well suited to their skills, knowledge base, values, aspirations or any combination of these. Consider the following real but anonymized examples:

- Edith enjoyed her work in a long-time child care team, but was unhappy with the poor supervision and lack of leadership offered by the team manager. As a result of these concerns she applied for, and got, a job in an intake team with a manager who had an excellent reputation. However, despite the major improvement in management, she did not enjoy the short-term, rapid turnover nature of intake work. She was extremely unhappy in the role and started to feel stressed. Within nine months she had moved to a long-term child care team, this time one with a good manager, and not only did the stress disappear, but she also began to flourish.

- Zaf had always wanted to be involved in training, so he was delighted when he was successful in his application for a workforce development officer post. However, he had not realized that he would have very little opportunity to be involved in direct training provision. Most of his time was involved in planning, organizing, coordinating and handling the financial management of training, rather than actually delivering it. He found working life a real struggle, as this was not what he wanted to be doing. Within less than a year he had left his post to become a team leader back in practice. He still wanted to be involved in training, but he knew he would need to look for opportunities elsewhere.

- Sheila was a family support worker who loved her job. However, after completing her social work training on a part-time basis, she was given a post in a child protection team. This meant that she actually spent relatively little time with the children or their families and a lot of time in meetings and working at the computer. She got to the point where she was considering going back to a family support worker post, even though this would mean a drop in salary. At least, she thought, she would be a lot happier in that role. She mentioned this to her manager in supervision and he encouraged her to stick at her present role for a while to get more experience and then, when ready, start applying for more specialist therapeutic roles where she could be more directly involved with families.

In developing your plan, it is extremely important to get a full picture of what would be involved in any role you are considering working towards. For example, we know of people who had aspirations to work in a university setting, but on achieving their ambition, they quickly realized that the culture in an academic institution is so different from what they had known and so different from what they would like it to be, that they no longer felt comfortable or even safe in such an environment. This is just one example of the type of error that can so easily be made if insufficient planning is done, by which we mean failing to get a full enough picture of what the particular role will entail on a day-to-day basis.

Another example would be the people we have come across who have gone into a management position because they enjoy supervising staff, only to realize that they struggle to make time for such activities because so much of the pressure upon them is around attending meetings and managing budgets.

It is also important to consider potential career blockages. What are the obstacles that may stand in the way of you achieving what you set out to? For example, would you need a particular qualification you do not yet have? Is there a gap in your experience that may mean that you would struggle to be appointed to a role that is part of your career plan? Some may be easily removed or circumnavigated; others may prove more difficult; and yet others may prove to be immovable.

There may be other factors to consider as well. For example, if you live and work in a rural area, would part of your plan necessitate at some point moving to an urban area and, if so, will this be acceptable to your family (if you have one) and would this matter to you in terms of your quality of life? This is not to say that you should rule out any such potential openings, but you do need to be aware that certain career paths may present obstacles that you had not anticipated.

The spiritual basis of career development

When we talk of spiritual issues, we need to stress again that we are not necessarily talking about religion. As we have already noted, not everybody is religious, but everyone has spiritual needs and faces spiritual challenges. Managing our career plans wisely and effectively is part of that sphere of spiritual challenges. There is no shortage of people who have traded material benefits at the expense of losing out in spiritual terms. So, we are not necessarily encouraging you to engage with religion in any way, but we do wish to emphasize that many of the issues – not least career planning – that relate to surviving and thriving really are spiritual in nature.

Once we get past the simplistic notion of a career as simply a process of climbing a metaphorical ladder, we can begin to see the links with spirituality much more clearly. Consider the following key elements of spirituality:

- *A sense of who we are and how we fit into the wider world* In a very real sense, this is what a professional career is all about. Our work is very much a part of our identity for most people. Having a career (rather than just a series of different jobs) contributes considerably to our sense of who we are, of what we are committed to and what direction we see ourselves heading in. It also says something about how we fit into wider society, what role we play in the overall scheme of social organization. For example, social workers play a key role in making our society a humane one as far as we reasonably can; small business owners play a part in keeping the economy going; police officers play a part in maintaining law and order. That is, work. in these terms, is not simply a means of earning a living. Each role plays a part in the wider society, and so in adopting a particular career, we are not just addressing our own needs at a micro level, but also being an element in the configuration of wider society at a macro level.

- *A sense of purpose and direction* The very idea of career development can be seen as precisely a matter of purpose and direction. When we make a career move, we are not just taking our work in a particular direction, we are also taking our lives in that direction. We are shaping our future in significant ways. In a sense, we are making a statement (whether we intend to or not) about what we see as our purpose, as what we are trying to achieve in (and with) our lives.

- *Connectedness* In spiritual terms, connectedness means having a sense of connection, especially to something greater than ourselves. In choosing a career in social work, we are, in a sense, recognizing and affirming a connection to wider humanitarian aims. If we are taking our professionalism seriously, then we should be acutely aware of this aspect of our career choice – it is not (or should not be) just a matter of putting food on the table and paying our bills. It is about having a sense of being part of a much bigger enterprise around empowerment, social justice, protecting vulnerable people and so on. Unfortunately, though, the grinding pressures of the day-to-day realities of the job can mean many people lose sight of this important aspect of our spirituality.

- *Values* We have already emphasized the importance of values as an underpinning of practice, but they are, of course, also spiritual matters (Moss and Thompson, 2020). They shape, and are shaped by, our career choices. So much of what we do is influenced by our values, and our career is no exception.

- *Flourishing* There is so much being spoken and written about well-being and spirituality these days. Indeed, the term 'spiritual well-being' is being used more and more. However, in a sense, well-being (defined as quality of life) is not enough. What we need to aim for is *flourishing*. There is a parallel here with surviving and thriving. If we think of well-being as the equivalent of surviving – that is, achieving an acceptable quality of life – then we can see flourishing as the equivalent of thriving – achieving the best possible, rather than the just about satisfactory.

The linking thread, of course, is *meaning*. It is through these different aspects of spirituality that we create and sustain meaning in our lives. In making decisions about our career, we should therefore consider the spiritual implications of what is involved. This, of course, is far more significant than a narrow ladder-climbing mentality.

Conclusion

When it comes to surviving in a highly pressurized workplace where the danger of being overwhelmed is ever-present, many people find it helpful to have a longer-term plan. This is by no means necessary, but it clearly works for some people.

What we have tried to emphasize in this chapter is that a reliance on the common simplistic notion that career is all about ambition and climbing the ladder is unhelpful and unwise.

It is far more helpful to think more holistically about your career. If it suits you to climb to the next rung on the ladder, then we would certainly not discourage you from doing so, but we would certainly discourage you from uncritically assuming that this is all there is to career development.

As we have emphasized, the key issue is balance, particularly the balance between what is to be gained by moving up a rung and what could potentially be lost. In addition, there is the important balance between what promotion can offer in a materialistic sense in terms of higher income and status against the more spiritual elements in terms of health, well-being and happiness, values and sense of connection to be gained from a less well-paid job, but one that is much better suited to you and your needs.

Chapter 9: Work-Life Balance

Introduction

The topic of work-life balance is one that has received a lot of attention over the years. Given the detrimental changes in the world of work that we outlined in Chapter 1, this is perhaps not surprising. The term itself is not a helpful one because it implies that work and life are two different things, rather than the former forming part of the latter. As Smith and Smith (2008, p. 118) point out, it is: 'an odd phrase carrying, as it does, the notion that work is somehow outside of life'. None the less, the issues the concept raises are very real and very significant, and certainly worthy of our attention – hence a whole chapter dedicated to exploring them.

The basis of the concept is the recognition that individuals in the workplace will also have to manage pressures from other aspects of their lives. It is often the combination of home-based pressures and workplace pressures that leads to people struggling to manage what is being asked of them in both domains. What complicates matters is that this is not simply an additive relationship, but more often a multiplicative one. By this we mean that it is not simply a matter of totting up some notion of a quantity of pressure. It is more a case of recognizing how the two sets of pressures can interact and make each other worse. We shall discuss this particular point in more detail below, but for now, we want to highlight that the relationship between the two domains is not a straightforward one.

We will be exploring five sets of issues. First of all, we will consider what is involved in seeking to establish a balance between what is demanded of us in the workplace and what demands come to us in our personal lives. We tackle this under the heading of 'Easier said than done' because that is precisely what it is – an important, but very difficult, undertaking. Second, we shall explore the significance of self-care and resilience, two concepts that have also been receiving a lot of attention for some time now, but which are often prone to oversimplification. As is so often the case when a topic becomes 'flavour of the month', people tend to look for or offer simple answers to complex problems. We will therefore be highlighting the need to appreciate the complexities involved.

Following this, we will revisit the theme of spirituality, with the notion of self-leadership as a key part of this. To what extent we are able to take hold of our lives and move it in the direction we want to go is very much a spiritual matter, and also very much a factor when it comes to trying to achieve work-life balance. Fourth, we shall return to our theme of the interaction of the micro and macro levels. As in our earlier discussions, we will be emphasizing the need to look holistically at the situation, incorporating both micro-level and macro-level factors, rather than focusing narrowly on one at the expense of the other. Finally, we shall explore the significance of work-life balance in the context of a growing emphasis on workplace well-being as a necessary basis for organizational success.

Easier said than done

By its very nature, working life brings pressures. In a sense, this is what we are being paid for, to address those pressures and demands on the part of our employer with a view to helping the organization to achieve its goals. If no demands were being made of us, no one would be prepared to pay us, of course.

However, as we have already seen, the current state of play in the modern workplace (and especially in social work) is highly problematic for a number of reasons, not least due to the pervasive influence of neoliberal thinking that is particularly inimical to social work. Monbiot (2016), in his insightful analysis of modern society, captures the point well:

> The workplace has been overwhelmed by a mad, Kafkaesque infrastructure of assessments, monitoring, measuring, surveillance and audits, centrally directed and rigidly planned, whose purpose is to reward the winners and punish the losers. It destroys autonomy, enterprise, innovation and loyalty, and breeds frustration, envy and fear.
>
> (pp. 16-17)

What this tells us is that any adequate understanding of the current work scene needs to take account of not only the pressures that are intrinsic to working life, but also the extrinsic pressures that have arisen in recent years. In other words, we must not underestimate just how pressurized modern workplaces can be.

So, that is one side of the equation, the workplace. The other is our life outside of work, our home life, for want of a better term. Home and family life can be a great source of solace and support, a safe haven to which to return from the rigours of working life. However, it would be naïve not to recognize that family life can also be a source of significant pressures, whether ongoing demands arising for various reasons (such as tensions within the family around one or more issues) or one or more specific pressures that may be to the fore at that particular time (for example, caused by illness or other family disruption, such as a bereavement).

Someone who is perfectly capable of dealing with their work pressures in normal circumstances may struggle to keep things going if, at a particular time, they also have a further range of home-based pressures to contend with. Consider the following two examples:

- Sam was coping well with work pressures, despite having quite a high caseload and lots of complex cases. However, one day she learned that her father had died. She had had a difficult relationship with her mother but was very close to her father. The very next day her sister was involved in a serious road traffic accident, perhaps due to her grief affecting her ability to drive safely. The net result was that Sam had to be persuaded to take time out from work as she felt so overwhelmed with really difficult emotions that she was temporarily in no position to practise safely.

- Yusuf had just successfully completed his probationary period and was delighted with the very positive report he had received. He was confident, had a supportive line manager and was at the top of his game. However, the situation changed drastically when his wife was diagnosed with breast cancer. It had been caught early enough for the prognosis to be good, but it was still a major worry and a big disruption of family life. Shortly afterwards, his son, possibly more tense than usual because of his mother's cancer diagnosis, was suspended from school after punching a white boy who had racially abused him. He did not know which was more disappointing, that his son had been racially abused or that he had responded with violence, despite having been brought up to eschew violence. The combination of these pressures meant that Yusuf had to talk to his manager about reducing his workload for a while so that he did not become overwhelmed.

While managers are not expected to help employees manage their home pressures, they do at least need to be aware of any such matters that may put the employee at risk in terms of health and safety due to a dangerous combination of home-based and work-based pressures. Line managers therefore need to be not only aware of any unusual home pressures, but also prepared to make allowances and offer support as appropriate.

What can be particularly trying is when there are additional pressures in both domains at the same time, home and work – for example, when there are more than the usual pressures at home in family life due to personal and familial circumstances, while at the same time additional pressures in the workplace (such as staff shortages or some reason why there is an unusually high level of pressure at a particular time). Imagine, for example, if, instead of persuading Sam to take some time out, her manager had said that, due to staff shortages, not only could there be no time out, but she was actually due to be allocated some more cases. Or, imagine if Yusuf had not yet passed his probationary period and he had an unsupportive manager who took no account of his personal circumstances in evaluating the quality of his practice in relation to whether or not he was to pass his probationary period.

In addition, we need to take account of the interactive nature of the two sets of pressures. We mentioned earlier that the term work-life balance is misleading in a sense because it implies that work is not part of life. We can also see, though, that the notion of balance is perhaps not the ideal term either. This is because it implies that we need a simple balancing out process between the two sets of pressures. The reality is that each set of pressures can have an adverse effect on the other. For example, a worker who is the parent of a teenaged son or daughter who is currently presenting problems within the family home may be so tense, worn out and distracted that they struggle to concentrate and focus fully on their work. In parallel fashion, someone who is being bullied in the workplace may take their pent-up feelings home with them and take out their frustrations on their family, thereby creating additional problems in the home domain.

Regrettably, neither of these scenarios is unusual. People will often be trying to cope with the range of pressures, and it will often be the dynamic interplay of those pressures that can lead to a vicious circle that proves to be too much to handle at that particular time. For example, had Sam not taken time out, her intense feelings of grief may have led her to not tune in to the emotional dimension of the work she was doing with clients. This could possibly have led to a complaint being made against her. The pain, embarrassment, anxiety and overall pressure of the complaint could have left her with no emotional energy to support her injured and grieving sister, with the potential for conflict between them to develop.

Similarly, had Yusuf's anxiety reached the level where he had become absentminded about his work and had neglected to do some important things, leaving himself open to criticism and in fear of failing his probationary period, he may have become a very short-tempered parent. If that had led to his losing his temper with his son, this could have been very detrimental for his son and for Yusuf himself when he later felt extremely guilty and ashamed of 'flying off the handle'.

With both of these examples, we are, of course, back in vicious circle territory, with potentially disastrous consequences. Clearly, then, both employers and employees need to be tuned in to the challenges of work-life balance and to be as well equipped as possible to manage them effectively.

These examples give the lie to the idea that stress is the sign of a weak individual. Employees who show signs of stress may be facing insurmountable levels of pressure due to the complex interactions and mutual reinforcement of different sets of pressures. Once again, we need to emphasize that employers are not expected to take any responsibility for home-based pressures, but their health and safety duties mean that, if they are aware that there is a danger that the interaction of pressures from the two domains is placing the employee's health and well-being at risk, they are obliged to take the matter seriously.

Equally, the individual's own health and safety responsibilities mean that it is essential to be open about such matters. Employers cannot be legitimately criticized for failing to offer appropriate support if they are not made aware of what the individual employees are currently going through. Making your employer aware is known technically as 'putting them on notice'. If you are under levels of pressure that are putting your health and well-being and your ability to do your job safely at risk, then it is your duty to make this matter known to the appropriate people within your organization, usually your direct line manager. You are not necessarily obliged to reveal confidential matters, although you may feel it helpful to do so if you trust the person concerned sufficiently. You will, though, need to share the fact that you are currently in a situation where you are under immense and potentially dangerous levels of pressure.

We are aware of many real-life situations where overworked managers have not noticed their staff are under undue pressure and their staff, not wishing to rock the boat or to be labelled as 'not coping' have not raised their concerns. Of course, two wrongs do not make a right, and so these highly unsatisfactory situations can do a lot of harm to all concerned.

The most effective micro-level way of dealing with so-called work-life balance is what is known as 'compartmentalization'. This refers to the ability to keep the two domains separate as far as possible. The best-case scenario is training yourself to focus on work-based pressures when you are at work and to put your home-based pressures in abeyance during that time. Similarly, you should be able to focus on your home-based pressures when you are at home and put your work-based pressures in abeyance. This is why this is referred to as compartmentalization, because you are basically putting the two sets of pressures in separate compartments, so that you can deal with each of them in turn on their own terms at the appropriate time. This involves a degree of self-awareness and self-control, skills that can take time to develop if you are not already very competent in those areas.

The worst-case scenario is when someone is at home struggling to deal with their home-based pressures because they are focusing so much on their work-based pressures precisely at the time when they are not in a position to do anything about them. Vice versa, people can be focusing on their home-based problems when at work and therefore not paying sufficient attention to their work challenges. This mismatch can be potentially disastrous. But, there is also the potential for disaster in trying to focus on both sets of pressures at the same time, regardless of whether you are at home or at work. This is a recipe for overloading yourself.

The reason this section of the chapter is entitled 'easier said than done' is that we recognize that many people find this type of compartmentalization very difficult. Some lucky people have no difficulty at all, as they are very effective at drawing the line between the two domains. For example, some people have told us that, although having a long commute to their place of work can be a source of pressure in its own right, it can also help with compartmentalization. That is, they use the journey as a boundary marker, drawing an important line between the two domains. By the time they get to work each morning they have had chance to switch off from the home-based pressures and, likewise, their journey home each evening gives the opportunity to, as it were, get work issues out of their hair before arriving home.

Other people use other compartmentalization techniques, such as having a shower or changing their clothes when they get home from work as a way of signalling to themselves and their family members that the change of domain has happened. But, whatever the approach adopted, the important thing is being able to keep the two sets of pressures separate as far as reasonably possible, so that the chances of being overwhelmed by this combination of pressures is minimized.

Another way of handling work-life balance is to make sure that we keep matters in proportion. This too is easier said than done, but where we are able to manage it, it can make a significant difference. This brings us back to the theme of vicious circles. When people feel pressurized, they get tense; when they are tense, they can start to worry; when they worry, there can be a tendency to lose perspective. What happens then is that the demands and challenges can loom larger than they are and make it difficult for us to keep things in proportion. This is where support can prove beneficial, especially where it involves having a trusted confidant who is able to play an important role in helping us to keep our feet on the ground and retain that important sense of perspective. In this respect, people who tend to keep their concerns to themselves and bottle them up are taking unnecessary risks by not asking for support. Having a sense that we are on our own and unsupported is likely to sap confidence, increase anxiety and thereby make it more likely that we will experience stress.

This takes us back to the theme of our own personal responsibility to highlight difficulties we are experiencing and to seek appropriate support. Bottling things up is a dangerous strategy and people who tend to do this can be seen to be at a higher level of risk. There can be a significant irony here, in the sense that, as social workers, we will often be encouraging family members to talk openly about their concerns, difficulties and worries, so that they are better placed to address them, and yet in terms of our own challenges, many of us will not follow our own advice and will be reluctant to share such issues. 'Physician, heal thyself' comes to mind as an analogy.

Once again, this is a reflection of the pathologizing model of stress that sees it as a reflection of a weak or inadequate individual. Such a model can make people reluctant to express their anxieties and concerns, thereby preventing them from being in a stronger position to rise to the challenges involved

Self-care and resilience

It is now widely accepted that we are in no position to look after others if we are not looking after ourselves. If we are too tired, too distracted, too stressed, too focused on just surviving, then what we can offer others by way of care, support, protection and empowerment is going to be significantly limited, while also putting ourselves at risk of burnout by overstretching ourselves. Often these problems arise because of some of the issues we have already addressed, namely a lack of assertiveness that leads to people allowing themselves to be overloaded and/or a failure on our part to set out our stall and clarify what can reasonably be achieved in any given set of circumstances.

Self-care involves the basics of making sure that we are eating well, exercising, getting enough sleep and generally making sure that we are not placing undue physical strain on our bodies that will have a knock-on effect on our mental and emotional capabilities. However, these basics are not enough on their own. We also need to make sure that we are not taking on so much work that we do not give our heart and mind enough time to recuperate after the exertions of our work. We also need to make sure that we have enough personal resources left over to be able to handle the emotional challenges of the work.

Allcorn (2005) makes the important point that: 'The workplace is saturated with our humanity' (p. 21) and adds that: 'the workplace is filled with the complexity of humanity' (p. 233). What this means is that workplaces can be very challenging places in general, but we can also note that the social work workplace is particularly demanding, especially in emotional terms.

At times, these challenges can be quite extreme – for example, working with a child who was being severely abused and/or supporting people through a major grief reaction following a significant loss. We are not robots who can turn off our feelings, however objective and dispassionate we try to be. We therefore have to be realistic about our own emotional needs.

Ironically, even in the caring professions where there is an expectation that people will be gentle and compassionate, a macho approach to pressures is widely prevalent. This appears to be a sort of misplaced stoicism where people believe that by 'being tough', they are preparing themselves well for the rigours of the job. Papadatou (2010) talks about being 'vulnerable enough'. This means being sufficiently in touch with our own existential vulnerability to be sensitive and empathic, but not allowing the extent of vulnerability to become debilitating. Achieving such a balance also goes under the heading of 'easier said than done', but it is none the less always the aim to pursue. It is an example of what is often called 'self-compassion'.

In some ways, resilience has become something of a buzzword. Part of this has been a tendency in some quarters for it to be oversimplified. Thompson and Cox (2020) emphasize the importance of recognizing resilience as a sociological phenomenon – that is, one that is largely shaped by wider cultural and structural factors. The tendency to see resilience as something people either have or do not have, as if it is simply a personal characteristic, is both misleading and potentially dangerous, as it leads us back to a victim-blaming approach.

Resilience can be understood as the process of 'bouncing back' from adversity. When life's challenges knock us down, we can either stay down and lose out, or we can get back up again and continue our struggle. Ideally, resilience should take us beyond that, so it is not just a matter of bouncing back, but also learning, growing and benefiting from how we handled the adverse circumstances (an example of existential learning). As we noted in Chapter 6, this chimes well with some aspects of social work theory in terms of such matters as crisis intervention (Thompson, 2018d), post-traumatic growth (Calhoun and Tedeschi, 2006) and transformational grief (Schneider, 2012).

Given that so much of social work is about managing adversity, resilience can be understood as a key concept, in terms of both how nurturing it in the people we support can be of great value and nurturing it in ourselves can be a key factor in terms of moving from surviving to thriving. We therefore need to recognize the importance of resilience as a concept and a phenomenon, while also being aware of the common tendency of using it uncritically in a narrow individualistic way that serves to pathologize people in certain circumstances.

The spiritual dimension

We have already commented on our understanding of spirituality as a phenomenon that does not have to be understood in religious terms. To our mind, religion is just one way of expressing our spirituality. All of us, whether religious or not, are tasked with finding meaning, purpose and direction in our lives, while having a sense of connectedness to other people and to wider concerns and causes. If we do not take account of the fact that so many of the issues raised in this book have their roots in spiritual challenges, we are missing a highly significant dimension of the workplace challenges and our attempts to tackle the issues that form the basis of our subject matter.

In our view, central to this is self-leadership, by which we mean the practice of establishing a sense of direction in our lives and making sure that we are doing what we need to do to keep on track with that direction. It is about having goals, about keeping in touch with our values and making sure that our mindset is consistent with both what we are trying to achieve and the ethical base of what informs our actions.

To what extent we are able to practise self-leadership effectively will be very significant in determining how successful we are in managing the challenges of maintaining an appropriate balance of home and work pressures.

The materialistic emphasis of modern societies tends to marginalize spiritual concerns, limiting them to either the religious domain (and thereby failing to address the growing numbers of people who are not members of faith communities) or to what tend to be seen as eccentric, such as 'New Age' groups or equivalent. Spirituality as a day-to-day concern for *everybody* is only just beginning to be appreciated. So much of what matters spiritually tends to be subsumed under popular psychology labels, such as 'self-help' or 'personal development' and therefore tends to be:

(i)   *Oversimplified*, with little or no appreciation of the complexities involved;

(ii)   *Commodified* – that is, treated as business opportunities, rather than as reflections of basic human needs (which is how much of the oversimplification arises); and

(iii)   *Individualized*, with little or no consideration of wider organizational, cultural or structural factors.

If we are to be serious about striking an effective work-life balance, then we need to engage with the idea that what we are wrestling with are profound spiritual matters (in the sense that we are using spiritual here), and not straightforward technical matters that can be managed superficially.

Given this important spiritual dimension, we need to make sure that our efforts to achieve work-life balance take account of spiritual elements, such as meaning, purpose, direction, values, connectedness and a sense of who we are and how we fit into the world. Keeping these issues in mind should help to 'ground' us and help to keep stress and burnout at bay.

Macro and micro

Addressing the challenges of work-life balance connects us once again with our macro/micro theme. Much of the literature on work-life balance has been narrow and individualistic in its focus, risking feeding a victim-blaming approach. A more holistic approach helps us to realize that, while micro-level factors have a part to play, and often a very significant part, they are by no means the whole story. We also need to bring into the picture the significance of wider factors, such as the problems associated with inadequate working conditions, a lack of support and/or unrealistic expectations of us, as we have already discussed.

We also need to do our best, if we are to take work-life balance seriously, to move away from a pathological model of stress and appreciate that the reality of the situation is far more complex than a simple reflection of somebody who is not able to 'cut it' in difficult times.

As we noted in Chapter 5, assertiveness and the ability to negotiate expectations in the form of 'setting out our stall' also have a part to play at the micro level. If we become particularly skilful at these elements, one of the bonuses is that they can play a part in shaping the macro level – for example, by influencing policy development, team functioning and, to a certain extent at least, quality of leadership.

Johnson (2004) highlights the importance of the macro level, recognizing that there is more to positive work experiences than encouraging workers to look after themselves. As he puts it:

> The real truth is simple: work-life balance isn't working. People – your employees – have come up with a different way of looking at it. It's called life-work balance. Life first, work later. And this is what is going to drive the new social contract between employer and employee.
>
> (p. 3)

This helps us to recognize that, while the micro level is important and individuals do have a degree of responsibility for self-care, it needs to be understood in the context of the wider macro level where organizational factors need to be seen as important in shaping experiences of working life.

Davies (2012), in his study of the important role of suffering in social life, also pinpoints the need to look beyond the micro level:

> Freud believed that if we were out of step with our society, somehow we were at fault. For Freud we suffered not because our social environment inhibited our unique needs and talents, but because we were inadequate to the demands of our society. For example, he believed that women who suffered from hysteria in 1990s Vienna did not do so because at that point in history, women were socially oppressed (i.e. because their suffering was a protest against the social oppression), but because they were afflicted by

certain internal psychological problems which required treatment.

(pp. 35-6)

Cederström and Spicer (2015) echo this sentiment when they are critical of the proselytizing of Jamie Oliver on healthy eating for school children. They point out the narrow focus of his thinking that takes no account of wider issues in children's lives, such as poverty and oppression.

We need to be crystal clear, then, that the emphasis on self-care, resilience, work-life balance and assertiveness needs to be understood as part of a micro-macro dynamic (a dialectic), and not in isolation in an atomistic sense.

Workplace well-being

Welch, a well-known writer in the business world, has emphasized the need to treat people with dignity and give them voice (Welch, 2001). It is ironic that someone from the harsh and competitive world of business should provide such an important message that needs to be heeded in the caring professions, including social work. That is, the fact that social work is built on a foundation of care and compassion does not mean that people will necessarily be treated with care and compassion. Both authors are very familiar, through our respective professional roles, with many examples of employees not being treated with dignity or given a voice (hence the importance of professional organization and trade union support).

We cannot, therefore, assume that the status of social work as one of the 'caring professions' in any way guarantees a supportive and humane working environment.

The emphasis on workplace well-being that has become so much to the fore in recent years (Kinder *et al.*, 2008; Thompson and Bates, 2009) therefore needs to be applied as much to social work settings as to any other.

Although some people have tried to use the notion of workplace well-being cynically and manipulatively, it remains an important basis for both surviving and thriving. Where it works well and is it is carried out in a spirit of partnership and empowerment, workplace well-being creates win-win outcomes, in the sense that all involved can benefit. As Robertson and Tinline (2008) explain:

> Psychological well-being [PWB] is the platform for low rates of sickness absence, optimal levels of employee turnover and high productivity. It is worth emphasising that the reaction of employees to a PWB initiative is likely to be positive – because the aim is to make them feel good at work. This is very different from some types of initiatives that are designed to improve organisational performance and which often elicit more guarded, or even actively negative, reactions. This is another facet of the benefits associated with pursuing a PWB approach.
>
> (p. 48)

There is therefore much to be gained from seeing work-life balance not simply as another means of blaming the victim, but as part of the complex phenomenon of workplace well-being where both employees and employers share a responsibility for creating and sustaining positive and productive workplaces where people feel supported, valued and safe.

The issue of safety is doubly important. There is the sense in which we have already used it, namely the conventional idea of health and safety – earthed electrical goods, warning signs on recently mopped floors and so on. However, there is also the sense of emotional safety. Costello (2020) connects it with issues of trust and feeling valued:

> When we feel valued and trusted in the workplace, our sense of feeling secure is high because we feel safe. We feel confident about expressing our thoughts and feelings openly and clearly, and we are usually ready and indeed seek to negotiate compromises about what to do about problems. yet when circumstances change and things feel risky, such as at times of restructuring, or when working with people we do not know who may not have our best interests at heart, we choose other, more guarded strategies.
>
> (pp. 46-7)

This is why blame cultures are so destructive; they undermine trust, feeling valued and, in particular feeling safe. When people feel unsafe, they will not be able to fulfil their potential, they will be much less creative or innovative and their ability to learn will be reduced. Safety, in this latter sense, is therefore an important component of workplace well-being.

Unfortunately, the notion of commodification that we touched on earlier has played a part in oversimplifying and trivializing some very important issues through commercialization. Popular culture now gives a strong message that you can buy happiness and well-being through pills, potions and lifestyle consumer goods.

Cederström and Spicer, in an important work that challenges this tendency, introduce the notion of 'biomorality' which they define as: 'the moral demand to be happy and healthy' (2015, p. 5). This fits with the work of Davies (2012) we mentioned earlier, with its emphasis on the role of suffering in meaning making (and thus spirituality). Any expectation that we can be happy and healthy at all times is clearly very wide of the mark. We therefore need to be wary of this tendency to individualize, commercialize and oversimplify the notion of well-being.

Thompson (2019c) helps us to appreciate what is involved in an understanding of workplace well-being that does not fall foul of such a reductionist approach:

> A commitment to workplace well-being involves the following key features:
> - Making sure that staff (and managers) feel valued and supported, with the benefits of effective leadership.
> - Protecting all employees from 'toxic' experiences (stress; bullying and harassment; aggression and violence; and so on).
> - Recognizing that, where there are people, there will be problems, and being prepared to address these problems constructively and supportively, rather than simply brushing them under the carpet. Such problems include: conflicts; drug and alcohol problems; loss, grief and trauma; mental health problems and so on. If such problems are not recognized and dealt with, the result is likely to be higher levels of sickness absence, recruitment and retention problems and a reduction in the quality and quantity of work.
>
> Given the importance of work in the lives of so many people, we can see that

workplace well-being is a very significant set of considerations and one worthy of careful attention.

(p. 13)

We therefore need to be sure that we are not relying on a misleading approach to well-being and work-life balance that places the onus solely on the shoulders of individual employees. The reality is much broader and much more complex than that.

Conclusion

We have covered a lot of ground in a relatively small space, and so in some ways we have only just begun to cover the topic, leaving a number of other aspects unsaid for further study and reflection. However, we trust that what we have presented here will be helpful in terms of developing your understanding of what has come to be known as work-life balance, which for the most part means making sure that the dynamic interplay of pressures in the two domains of work and home do not result in an unmanageable level of pressure.

We regard getting stuck in some of the many vicious circles that are part and parcel of the contemporary workplace as problematic enough. But, when we add vicious circles that develop from interactions between the work and home domains, we start to see just how significant the challenge of managing some sort of work-life balance is.

An important part of reflective practice is the ability to take a step back, review where we are up to and decide then, on the basis of our professional knowledge, skills and values, how best to proceed. In the business world, an important principle that is often emphasized is that owners of successful businesses know how to work *on* the business as well as *in* the business. That is, they are able to look at the business more holistically, identify strengths to build on and weaknesses to address, so that they can develop a strategy for moving forward as positively and successfully as possible. We are well aware that much of the problematic nature of the social work world today has its roots in the neoliberal tendency to fail to appreciate the significant differences between public service work and running a business. However, this is one exception where a business analogy is actually quite useful. Someone trying to run a business who just focuses on the day-to-day management of the business and loses sight of the bigger picture of where the business is going, what needs to happen, and so on is placing the business at significant risk. This takes us back to our theme of self-leadership. If we are not taking the time to step back and look holistically at work-life balance, there is a very real danger that the combination of pressures will overwhelm us and bring about highly detrimental consequences.

Once again, we have placed emphasis on understanding micro-level issues, macro-level factors and the interactions between the two. We have also seen how it can be helpful to seek to understand work-life balance in a wider context of workplace well-being. In so doing, we avoid the pathologizing tendency to see work-life balance and workplace well-being as purely individual responsibilities.

Chapter 10: Making it Happen

Introduction

We trust we have made it clear throughout that there are no magic answers or some simple formulas to follow when it comes to surviving today's highly demanding social work environment and working towards making thriving as much of a reality as possible. However, this does not mean that there is no useful guidance that we can give you based on our decades of experience of offering training and consultancy on these issues and being engaged in trade union support activities. We have covered a lot of ground in this book and each chapter has covered a set of important issues. In this final chapter our aim is to bring together the key lessons to be learned in terms of trying to make surviving and thriving a reality.

The chapter is divided into three main sections. In the first one we explore some key strategies that can be used in order to maximize the chances of survival and lay important foundations for working towards thriving. These are not guaranteed to work, of course, but they should significantly increase your chances of obtaining positive outcomes from your efforts. In the second part we explore a range of pitfalls to avoid. These refer to mistakes that we have seen people make over the years, pitfalls that can have significant detrimental consequences. We therefore offer a discussion of them in a spirit of 'forewarned is forearmed'.

In the third we revisit the Getting up to SCRATCH and BEYOND framework that we discussed in the Introduction in order to reinforce the importance of each of the elements that go to make up the two acronyms.

We hope that, in reading this chapter, you will be encouraged to put many of the ideas into practice. Simply knowing that there are strategies available and pitfalls to avoid will be of little or no use unless the lessons to be learned from these are drawn out and put into practice.

Some key strategies

There are many potential strategies that could be used but, for reasons of space, we are to focus on three in particular. The first of these is one that we have already commented on, namely self-management. How effective we are at managing pressures, people and ourselves will be a significant factor in determining the success or otherwise of our efforts. People will vary considerably in terms of how skilful and confident they are in such matters, but no one will be in a position where there is no room for improvement. We therefore encourage you to consider carefully our earlier discussion of self-management and our broader theme of self-leadership, so that you are, in effect, maximizing your chances of keeping your head above water in these difficult times.

Although in some ways it is possible to make quick gains in terms of self-management (for example, by making changes in how we communicate), the overall process of change is likely to be a gradual one. As each day, week, month and year pass, we can continue to build on our skills in this area. In doing so, we are putting ourselves in a much stronger position to break the vicious circles and to institute the virtuous ones that give us the potential to go from strength to strength.

It is difficult for us to give generic guidance about self-management skills because, although there are clear shared patterns, much will depend on the individual persona and circumstances of the practitioner concerned. Each of us will have our strengths and areas for development. So, what we want to encourage is greater self-awareness that enables us to identify as clearly as we can what the strong points are, so that we can build on them, while also acknowledging the not so strong points and developing a plan for addressing them, ideally being able to turn them into strengths too.

In a very real sense, self-management is a process of influencing ourselves – it involves reflectively standing back from our current circumstances and seeking to identify ways in which we can improve our functioning and get better results. Our second strategy builds on this, in so far as it retains the idea of influencing people, but this time influencing others, rather than ourselves. Our circumstances are not entirely in our own hands, but much will depend, of course, on the actions and attitudes of other people and our interactions with them. However, while we do not have complete control over these, nor do we have no sway in shaping what happens and what the end results are. That is, there is always scope for negotiation and the use of assertiveness. One tool that can be particularly helpful is what is known as the CIA framework, as discussed in Thompson (2019a). This framework has proven itself to be a very useful stress management tool.

The C stands for control. To use this tool all we need to do is identify those elements of the situation that we can control and make sure that this is precisely what we do, to make sure that whatever is within our power is managed as effectively as possible. Interestingly, people operating in high-pressure situations where there is a low-morale culture, will often be unduly negative and defeatist about what they can control. Consequently, when thinking about what we control, we have to make sure that we are not allowing such negativity to filter out important aspects of the situation that are actually within our control.

The I stands for influence. There will be many aspects of a situation that we cannot control, but which we can influence, to a certain extent at least. People tend to come within this category for the most part. That is, there may be few situations where we can directly control people, but opportunities to influence people arise all the time. This takes us back to the theme of assertiveness which involves developing the negotiation skills to secure win-win outcomes as far as possible. Unfortunately, many people struggle to make full use of assertiveness as an influencing skill, whether due to anxiety or any other such cause. The point remains, though, that not taking advantage of opportunities to influence situations in a positive direction can cost us dearly, as they make the likelihood of success in our endeavours much smaller.

The A stands for acceptance. In any given situation there will be some things that we can neither control nor influence, and so the wise response is to learn to accept them. If there is genuinely nothing we can do about a situation, then railing against it is likely to be counterproductive, especially if we continue to do this on a medium- to long-term basis. It is perfectly understandable that, where people feel frustrated about not being able to do anything about circumstances that they are unhappy with, they will struggle to 'let go'. However, if this venting of frustration continues for much longer, it can become highly problematic. It can contribute to low morale, as the focus continues to be on what we cannot do, rather than on what can. Not accepting things that we can neither control nor influence will sap our energy, create unnecessary tensions and generally make our task of surviving and thriving much more difficult.

The CIA framework can be a very useful tool, therefore, in terms of both self-management and influencing others. It can also be helpful in terms of our third strategy, namely, influencing the organization. Clearly, the more senior a person is in an organization, the more influence they are likely to have in terms of how the organization operates, its culture and so on. However, we need to be careful not to oversimplify this complex situation. It would be very easy to make the mistake of assuming that only senior personnel have the opportunity to influence what happens in an organization. We have noted that an important leadership skill is the ability to influence culture in a positive direction. However, it is not necessary to be in a senior position to be able to do so (although it definitely helps).

Thompson (2018c) discusses the notion of an 'organizational operator'. This refers to someone who has the skills, insights and sensitivity to be able to work out how to make a positive difference to the organization they work in. An organizational operator is someone who is able to recognize how power dynamics work and how they can be influenced. This is not an easy set of skills to develop, but they are worth pursuing none the less.

We should also not make the mistake of assuming that efforts to influence an organization need to be undertaken on an individual basis. Of course, this is where a collective approach comes into its own. There are different levels to this. For example, it may be a matter of a team pulling together to try and bring about some sort of change, whether that is a relatively minor change, right through to major cultural or structural rearrangements. Alternatively, it could be at a broader level – for example, through trade union activities where staff groups are acting collectively through their trade union structures, mechanisms and working agreements. Yet another, broader level would be where unions, professional organizations and other institutions potentially play a part in seeking to influence organizational functioning at a governmental level. That is, where there are concerted efforts to try and bring about changes in legislation, government guidance or other such macro-level factors as they affect organizational life.

The point we want to make is not that there are easy ways of influencing organizations, but rather that we should not exclude the possibility of doing so. Again, low-morale cultures that feed – and feed off – negativity defeatism and cynicism can be significant obstacles to people pulling together to support one another in seeking to bring about positive change.

In sum, then, when it comes to 'making it happen', these are just some of the strategies that can be used to bring about change through influence at individual and collective levels.

Pitfalls to avoid

As with the key strategies, there are far more pitfalls to avoid than we can realistically cover in one short chapter. We are therefore going to focus our attention on what we see as four particularly significant (and dangerous) pitfalls that are sadly quite common in the contemporary social work world.

The first we want to consider will come as no surprise, as it has featured significantly as a theme in many parts of the book. We are referring to the tendency to retreat into negativity, defeatism and cynicism. We fully appreciate how challenging and frustrating modern workplaces can be, particularly in social work in a context of a neoliberal devaluing of what social work has to offer. None the less, we do need to emphasize the dangers of such a negative mindset contributing to a low-morale culture. We have looked at the many highly destructive vicious circles that can so easily develop and which are so common. We have seen how these vicious circles can do significant harm and create many major problems for all concerned.

It is also not too difficult to see how negativity undermines professionalism. It is extremely difficult for people to retain a sense of professionalism when they have slipped into a mindset characterized by undue negativity. Such a mindset undermines confidence, distracts us from our values and can easily create a sense of futility. These are clearly not appropriate bases for developing, sustaining and celebrating the profession of social work. Here we encounter yet another vicious circle: negativity stands in the way of professional pride and the significant boost to morale it can bring; without that sense of professionalism, it can be difficult to sustain ourselves through the many challenges involved in social work; but struggling with those challenges can then undermine confidence and again feed negativity. The harmful cycle continues.

Losing sight of professionalism can also contribute to burnout. As we have noted, burnout is in some circumstances an understandable response to extremely challenging circumstances, but it is not a helpful one; it is self-defeating. A strong sense of professionalism that recognizes the value and importance of social work is a significant antidote to burnout. It serves as an important reminder of the key role social work plays in making our society a humane one.

Burnout can appear to be contagious, in the sense that, where there are one or more people experiencing burnout, a culture characterized by significantly low morale can emerge. This is then likely to have the consequence of dampening motivation for others and thereby further contribute to low morale and all the problems associated with it. This can then reinforce the reasons for the burnout that was being experienced in the first place.

A further pitfall that can arise because of burnout and which can also contribute to it is that of self-blame. The victim-blaming mentality that is sadly so common in relation to stress and the broader picture of coping with workplace and other pressures has the unfortunate effect of encouraging self-blame. Where people are unaware of the significance of the broader macro-level context, it is understandable that they fall back on explanations at the micro level. The sense of failure that this engenders is then likely to act as a spur to feelings of guilt, feelings to the effect that this is going wrong 'because of me'. This then encourages negative self-talk and the unhelpful assumption that what is going wrong is down to the individual concerned, rather than to the much wider holistic picture.

There are two important aspects of this that are worth commenting on more fully. The first one relates to the irony of the fact that, as social workers, we will regularly come into contact with people who are struggling to cope with their problems because of self-blame – the mother who blames herself for not being able to protect her child from the abusive attentions of a stepfather, for example; the person struggling with severe depression who is unduly harsh on him- or herself in terms of the circumstances that have contributed to the distress being experienced;

and/or the person with a drink-related problem who puts it all down to their own weakness or inadequacy. This self-blame and its role as an obstacle to progress are therefore something that we are very familiar with in social work. But this is yet another example of how applying what we know about other people's problems to our own concerns and challenges will often not happen. There is therefore very much to learn from seeing how we challenge other people's self-blame in order to try to address our own common problem within social work of allowing challenging circumstances to feed a sense of guilt and blame.

The second involves recognizing that a sense of guilt is common in situations where people are grieving. After a major loss, it is common for people to have a strong sense of 'if only I had done something differently', reflecting what is often referred to as 'pseudo-guilt'. It is called pseudo-guilt because, in the vast majority of situations, the grieving person has nothing to feel guilty about. However, the sense of helplessness and powerlessness that can be part and parcel of a grief reaction can generate feelings that are experienced by the individuals concerned as guilt. In social work we are commonly coming across grief at two levels. First, as we noted earlier, loss and grief issues are never far away in social work. Engaging with other people's feelings of grief can at times produce some degree of grief reaction in ourselves, of course. This can include a degree of pseudo-guilt that can then feed a sense of self blame.

Second, there can be a degree of grief when we are not able to achieve what we want to as professionals due to the current neoliberal restrictions, the absence of resources, a lack of support and appreciation or whatever. The 'moral distress' of struggling to practise within our value system also involves a degree of loss and therefore grief. It will not happen in every case, of course, but there will be occasions when the grief we experience feeds self-blame, especially in those circumstances where we do not realize that we are grieving and are therefore perhaps confused about what our feelings are telling us and where they are taking us.

Related to the theme of self-blame is that of self-sacrifice. This takes us back to our discussion of self-care and resilience. Social workers, along with other members of the caring professions, are likely to be 'other directed', which means that there is a danger that we put other people's needs before our own. While this is admirable in some ways in terms of a compassionate outlook on life, it also brings dangers, in so far as we can place ourselves in danger if we are overly other directed and thereby neglect our own needs. Sacrificing ourselves for the good of others may appear noble and worthy, but in very many circumstances it is a very unwise move. It brings us back to the important point made earlier that, if we are not looking after ourselves, we are in a seriously weakened position when it comes to caring for others.

Getting up to SCRATCH and BEYOND

As we noted earlier, to get up to scratch means to achieve an acceptable standard. We can therefore think of it as representing surviving. Aiming for thriving means doing more than just settling for surviving, which means going beyond just settling for surviving or getting by. We need to go beyond that bare minimum, hence the acronym of 'beyond'. Here we revisit each of the elements of the two acronyms and consider what part each of them can play in contributing to 'making it happen'.

*S*olidarity

Divide and conquer is generally a tactic of oppressive regimes, but even where division is not intended as a deliberate ploy, it will often happen when people find themselves in overpressurized circumstances. This is because a common defence mechanism in such circumstances is for individuals to withdraw into their own 'security bubble' where they hope they will feel safe. Ironically, this move is likely to put them at more risk of exploitation, as they lack the protection of fellow workers or of organized support (a trade union or professional organization, for example).

So, while a withdrawal strategy is understandable, it is less likely to be effective than joining forces with others who are similarly adversely affected by the shared circumstances. There is so much more that can be done on a collective basis in a spirit of solidarity. This does not mean that some degree of withdrawal to recharge our batteries or to recover from a hurtful or wounding experience is in any way a problem or something to be avoided. Rather, the problem arises when withdrawal becomes the primary or even sole way of trying to address the situation.

So, an important point to be aware of is this: when you find yourself struggling, the chances are that others too are in the same boat (although they may not readily show this if they fear evidence of struggling being seen as a sign of weakness, especially in a macho 'be tough' culture). It is therefore wise to think about solidarity, about how you can develop a collective response to collective challenges.

Caring for yourself

Being committed to doing a good job and trying to make sure that people's needs are as fully met as possible are admirable and worthy endeavours. However, it is essential that we do not allow these to come at the expense of our own health and well-being. We all have limits in terms of what we can achieve, how much of ourselves we can put into our work and how far we can go without proper rest and recuperation. Thompson (2019c), as one of the 101 tips he offers for optimal well-being, provides the following advice:

> Our muscles need time to recover from exertion before we exert ourselves further if we are not to strain them. The same applies to our mental and emotional 'muscles'. If we keep stretching ourselves in our work efforts (and in our lives more broadly) without giving ourselves time to recover, we run the risk of doing ourselves harm, potentially significant harm. Exertion plus recovery plus more exertion can produce growth and development (of muscles in the direct physical sense or of learning in our more metaphorical sense). Exertion followed by more exertion without recovery time in between can produce muscle strain and/or psychological stress. Time for recovery is therefore not an optional extra if we are to take our physical and mental health seriously.
>
> (p. 85)

Spreading ourselves too thinly or overstretching ourselves does not do anyone any good. Sadly, we have to emphasize this because problems associated with a lack of self-care we know to be quite common in social work. In our experience, they can arise for two main reasons:

1. Putting other people's needs before our own. Up to a point, this is not necessarily a problem in itself, but it can so easily become a major concern if we

allow this to go too far, resulting in a failure to address our own needs. Consider the (real) example of a social worker who left the house early to get to her office as soon as it opened because she had so much she wanted to get done that day; worked through her lunch break without even stopping for a quick sandwich; continued working until 7pm and, when driving home had a near-fatal car accident because she was so faint with hunger and fatigue that she lost concentration while driving. Not only did she almost die, she was also prosecuted for driving without due care and attention.

2. Allowing others to overload us. We are likely to have a far better idea of what we can and cannot manage in terms of a reasonable workload, but if we allow others to make those decisions for us (for example, if we choose not to be assertive), we run the risk of being overwhelmed by the demands being placed on us. Consider this (also real) example of a social worker who continued to accept new cases, even though she was already in a state of significant nervous tension and emotional distress because of her existing caseload, who ended up on stress-related sickness absence for several months. When asked why she had continued to accept cases, she said that she felt sorry for her manager who had so many cases to allocate, so she felt she 'couldn't say no'. On discovering what had happened, her manager was herself significantly distressed by what had happened and wished that she had been told of the difficulties so that she could be supportive. So, in terms of assertiveness, this had ended up as a 'lose-lose' outcome.

Reaffirming professionalism

We cannot expect others to take our professionalism seriously if we do not take it seriously ourselves, and yet it is not uncommon for social workers to allow themselves to get bogged down in bureaucracy and lose sight of the fact that, however much bureaucracy we have to wade through, we remain professionals. Social work is a professional endeavour in a bureaucratic context and not simply a set of bureaucratic processes. If we lose sight of our professionalism, it is then very easy to lose sight of the valuable contribution we make to society, our professional knowledge, skills and values and the professional pride we can take in making such an important difference (albeit often not as much difference as we would like to make) in such difficult circumstances.

Having a strong sense of professionalism and a strong commitment to our professional values can be a major source of motivation that can sustain us through difficult times and remind us about what it is all about when the going gets tough (or gets even tougher than usual).

Of course, we should not confuse a strong sense of professionalism with an elitist 'we know best' conception of professionalism. This is not about status, perks and privileges, it is about recognizing and constantly reaffirming the value of what we do and the key role of values in terms of how (and why) we do it.

Avoiding stress

Stress, in the sense of levels of pressure that do us harm in terms of our health, well-being, quality and quantity of work, relationships and so on, is a major problem in many workplace settings, and is particularly a challenge in social work for some of the reasons we have outlined. Based on the work of Thompson (2019a), we have noted that there are three elements that can be addressed to prevent or alleviate such stress:

- *Pressures* How do we keep them within manageable limits? This will involve being realistic about what we can reasonably achieve in the time and with the energy available to us and, where necessary, being appropriately assertive in negotiating a fair and reasonable workload.

- *Coping methods* How do we deal effectively with the pressures we face? We have various coping methods that we can draw upon, but it is essential that we do not allow the pressures to reach a level where we may become emotionally 'paralyzed' and then cease making use of those methods, temporarily at least.

- *Support* What sources of support, formal and informal, can we draw upon and, in a spirit of solidarity, what support can we offer? We need to move away from the very dangerous assumption that asking for support is a sign of weakness. We need to recognize it as a sign of a wise approach to managing the combination of home and work pressures.

Pressure is inevitable, but stress is not. We have to guard against the 'normalization' of stress whereby people start to assume that stress is an inherent part of social work and that we just have to learn to accept it. Stress is a sign that something is going wrong, and we need to understand that holistically in order to avoid victim blaming.

Theory driven

A high level of pressure can lead people to focus narrowly on just getting the job done pragmatically. Of course, while getting the job done is important, it has to be done properly, by which we mean professionally. That means drawing on our professional knowledge, skills and values. While under great pressure, people's minds can shut out our professional knowledge base, leaving us ill equipped to deal with the complex issues involved. In our experience, when cases go sadly wrong, it is often because important insights from our professional knowledge base were not taken into consideration – for example, working with older people without considering the significance of ageism (Sue Thompson, 2019).

Drawing on our theory base is an important part of professionalism and thus of both surviving and thriving. This tendency to bypass our theory base (and potentially our values) when under pressure is therefore a temptation that we need to strongly resist.

We also need to engage with our theory base not only in terms of direct practice, but also in relation to making sense of the current circumstances we face in social work in these neoliberal times. Indeed, this book is very much part of developing and highlighting that theory base.

We therefore need to avoid the tendency to see theory and practice as two separate worlds (a horizontal relationship) and, instead, recognize theory as underpinning practice (a vertical relationship) (Thompson, 2017b).

Challenging

'Elegant challenging' – that is, skilful, sensitive and tactful challenging – can make a very positive difference. Unfortunately, yet another vicious circle is common here. People who are under considerable pressure can lack the confidence to challenge aspects of a situation they are unhappy with. The lack of a challenge allows the unhappy situation to continue, and so the pressures continue. Confidence remains low and the challenge that needs to happen does not take place.

The significance of the notion of *elegant* challenging is important to recognize. Crude, aggressive, hostile or excessive challenging is likely to generate more problems than it solves by creating further distance, rather than bringing people closer together. The strong emotions generated by stressful situations can, unfortunately, lead to such unhelpful challenges, and so it is essential that we keep the notion of elegance in mind – that is, we make our challenges sophisticated, well-thought-out ones that are much more likely to be effective and bring about the changes we need. Basically, it is about being assertive, rather than aggressive.

Holistic approach

Looking at the big picture is, of course, a fundamental part of good practice in social work. If we get bogged down in the micro-level details and lose sight of the wider macro-level context, we run the risk of failing to recognize the impact of such destructive processes as racism, sexism, ageism and various other forms of discrimination and the oppression they give rise to (Thompson, 2021).

Once again, we need to apply the logic we use in direct practice in order to make sense of the challenges of surviving and thriving. As we emphasized in Chapter 3, we need to appreciate not only micro and macro factors, but also the complex interactions between them. This is, of course, a key part of the psychosocial approach that forms part of the basics of our practice.

Having considered getting up to SCRATCH and the part each element can play in surviving, we can now consider the BEYOND acronym and highlight what it means in terms of thriving.

Best practice

We earlier highlighted the problem of 'satisficing', which basically means settling for what is just about good enough. As we see it, an important element of professionalism is striving for the best possible outcomes, not lazily making do with the bare minimum required to avoid criticism or sanctions. We also see it as an importance element of both surviving and thriving.

In terms of surviving, trying to do the best we can in difficult circumstances can be an important source of motivation and can help sustain us through a range of challenges and difficulties. And, to go beyond surviving and on to thriving, aiming for optimal results has an important part to play.

Of course, we should not expect to get a 100% success rate, as that is just setting ourselves up to fail. But, what *is* realistic is to aim for best practice – that is, aiming to get the best results possible in constrained and challenging circumstances. Best practice is not about *getting* the best results, it is about being *committed to getting* the best results. There are far too many variables that we do not have control over to guarantee success, but we can guarantee that we will do our best – and we can take pride in that.

Empowerment

Empowerment is, or should be, a core element of social work. It is particularly important in terms of thriving for three reasons:

1. Returning to our theme of best practice, it should be clear that working in empowering ways wherever possible needs to be at the heart of what we do.

2. Earlier we discussed the way in which a vicious circle of self-disempowerment can arise, particularly in cultures characterized by low morale.

3. Empowerment can also be an important basis of management and leadership. As Huq (2015) argues:

    > Psychological empowerment not only paves the way for employees to develop their ability to empower themselves, enhance their locus of control, self-efficacy and self-esteem; it also needs to be highlighted that it has the potential to develop the abilities of leaders to reframe, de-skill and re-skill, enabling them to achieve psychological empowerment too, as there may be cases when leaders in [an] organisation lack self-efficacy and self-esteem.

Just because people are in management or leadership positions, it does not necessarily mean that that they automatically feel psychologically empowered.

(p. 219)

Huq's comments are important because basically they mean that managers can benefit in two ways from adopting an empowerment approach (getting the best out of their staff and being empowered in their own right). Employees (and other stakeholders) will also then be able to benefit. She goes on to give some useful guidance on how employee empowerment can be achieved:

> employee empowerment requires organisations to address a number of themes ... namely, power-sharing, participative decision-making, devolution of responsibility, people-oriented leadership style, access to information, collaboration and enablement ...

(p. 219)

Empowerment, with all it entails, is therefore a key concept when it comes to 'making it happen' in relation to making thriving a reality.

Yes saying

This is about affirmation. By its very nature, social work brings us into contact with pain, suffering, distress, grief, trauma and struggle. It is very easy, if we allow it to happen, to be dragged down into this mire and then be of little value to the people we are trying to support, while potentially doing a lot of harm to our own well-being and even our health.

'Yes saying' is not a simplistic 'look on the bright side' message. It is, rather, a serious and important way of avoiding the vicious circle of self-disempowerment that we discussed earlier. It is rooted in the idea of 'realism', in the sense that it is necessary, if we are to do justice to the complexity of human existence, to recognize both the positives and negatives of life. The nature of social work means that the negatives will generally be to the fore, but this means that it is all the more important that we counterbalance the negatives with positives – especially the positives associated with the important work we do and the significant impact we make in terms of making our society a humane one. We need to be the opponents of negativity, not its victims, difficult though that may be at times.

Understanding the nature of suffering can be helpful in this regard, as we recognized earlier. Davies's (2012) comments are once again insightful:

> no occurrence of suffering *arrives ready-made* as either 'productive' or 'unproductive'. Rather, suffering *becomes* either productive or unproductive depending upon how we manage and understand it *once it has arrived*. Its nature, in other words, is significantly shaped by how we respond to it. All rests, therefore, upon how it is understood and handled. As we have seen, if suffering is treated as a worthless experience to be removed or managed with what I have called anaesthetics, *it will inevitably become unproductive*. It will become unproductive simply because it is not being responded to in a way that can realise its productive meaning and worth.
>
> (p. 165)

Where we cannot alleviate suffering, therefore, we have an important role to play in trying to make it as productive (in Davies's terms) as possible, including our own suffering.

One for all and all for one

This takes us back to our solidarity theme. The need to support one another is not just a tactic for survival, it is also an important basis for thriving. The more we adopt a collective approach to our challenges, the stronger a position we will be in, the more support we will have, the more of a resource we will be to others and the more spiritually fulfilling our lives can be in terms of the role of 'connectedness'.

Neverending learning

Again, it is worth emphasizing that this is not simply a matter of ticking all the CPD boxes. This is about making a genuine commitment to maximizing our learning, to be proactive and self-directed in doing so, rather than allowing others to be in the driving seat. Every day brings new learning opportunities. We can capitalize on them or allow them to pass us by. The choice is ours to make, for each and every one of us.

Determination to succeed

No one can be blamed for being disheartened by the current state of social work within an underfunded, often hostile, neoliberal system. Staying motivated is quite a major challenge, but it is essential that we do, and that we support one another in doing so. We will, of course, often face failure, just as so many other people do in their own particular occupational setting (police, health professionals and so on), but giving up and giving in just makes a bad situation worse. By focusing on what we can do to be as successful as we reasonably can in difficult circumstances, by contrast, we are making a positive and worthwhile contribution.

Conclusion

We have acknowledged that this chapter is far from comprehensive; there is so much more that could be said about the issues covered here. However, what we hope this chapter will have achieved is the bringing together of some important points around positive and helpful strategies that can be used in our struggle to not only survive, but also to thrive, along with some insights about some of the many pitfalls that we need to be aware of, so that we do not make the mistakes that many of our predecessors have fallen foul of.

In keeping with one of the central messages of this book, we would want to emphasize very strongly that we need to move away from the idea that the problems so common in social work these days are a matter mainly for individuals. A collective response, rooted in a strong sense of solidarity, will put us in a much stronger position for tackling the many challenges that we face. When it comes to surviving, as in so many other aspects of life, we will be far better placed to do so if we are supporting one another and addressing our shared concerns in collective ways. This gives us far more power and influence, and also the benefit of making it safer for us as individuals in terms of the struggles we face.

Conclusion

As we are all very much aware, social work is not about easy answers. It is about the struggle to support, protect and empower people who are facing significant challenges in their lives. The broader circumstances they face, rooted in discrimination, oppression, alienation, poverty and myriad other discouragements are key parts of their story. In many circumstances, sadly, vicious circles develop that make the situation worse – for example, oppression contributes to depression; being seen as 'mentally ill' leads to stigma; stigma leads to discrimination; discrimination leads to oppression; and so on. The challenge in this type of situation is to resist getting drawn into the cycle or to break out of it if or when one does emerge.

There is a direct parallel here with the challenges of survival. For the various reasons we have explored throughout the book, the current situation is a highly challenging one for social workers, characterized by a number of vicious circles that can drag us down and wear us out. Our challenge, then, is likewise to avoid getting into such vicious circles where we can and doing our best to break out of them once they do arise. This is not necessarily easy, but it is important – vitally important, in fact – and, as we have been saying all along, it is better done collectively, with each of us supporting one another.

In many ways, we are swimming against the tide as a result of that tide at a political level going against social work values and, indeed, public services values more broadly. Swimming against the tide can be very discouraging – exhausting in fact – but it should be worth it if it means that we are making a positive difference to people's lives and, *importantly*, not doing so at the expense of our own health and well-being. What we must *not* do is internalize these difficulties as if they are signs of our own inadequacy. Monbiot (2016) offers some encouragement:

> So, if you don't fit in; if you feel at odds with the world; if your identity is troubled and frayed; if you feel lost and ashamed, it could be because you have retained the human values you were supposed to have discarded. You are a deviant. Be proud.

(p. 18)

Being a social worker in any age takes a lot of courage – especially moral courage – but especially so in these neoliberal times that are so hostile to the humanitarianism we stand for. Courage and pride go hand in hand, so we need to take pride in the important work we do and take courage from that.

In a later work, he goes on to offer helpful guidance in terms of what that would mean in practice:

> Where there is atomisation, we will create a thriving civic life. Where there is alienation, we will forge a new sense of belonging: to neighbours, neighbourhoods and society. Where we find ourselves crushed between market and state, we will develop a new economics that treats both people and planet with respect. Where we are ignored and exploited, we will revive democracy and retrieve politics from those who have captured it. ... I propose a name for this story: 'The Politics of Belonging'.
>
> (pp. 25-6)

In terms of our spirituality theme, perhaps we should think of belonging in terms of 'connectedness', the importance of feeling part of something bigger than ourselves and thus having deep connections to other people as part of a genuine sense of human connection.

Of course, we cannot do this alone. This is where solidarity comes into the picture, partly in terms of colleagueship and camaraderie at a team level, but especially at a national level – hence the importance of BASW in the UK and equivalent organizations in other countries. But, solidarity can be wider than that in terms of trade unionism as part of a national and international drive towards better working conditions and more worker-friendly workplaces – hence the importance of SWU.

Helen Keller, the author and humanitarian, was responsible for the famous comment that the world is full of suffering, but it is also full of the overcoming of it. This speaks so directly to the social work world, in terms of not only what we do in day-to-day practice, but also the challenges of promoting empowerment and social justice in a sociopolitical context that has a very different neoliberal agenda. Perhaps what we need to remember most of all is that alleviating suffering – and indeed preventing it where possible – is best done collectively. We really are in this together.

Afterword

Reading this accessible and powerful book, packed with constructive analysis and practical advice, has been a fruitful and energizing experience, helping to dispel some of the frustrations of the Covid-19 lockdown. The book is grounded in a pervading realism about the context of social work practice, particularly in the public sector, using a positive and optimistic approach to suggestions for surviving and thriving, which make sense and can make a difference.

My professional experience has included the privilege of observing and evaluating practice in a wide range of local areas in the UK as well as agencies around the world. As an Inspector in the Audit Commission, Ofsted and the Commission for Social Care Inspection, I have observed practice in getting on for half the local authorities in England and Wales. I discovered that, in almost every situation, however bad the context, there were invariably pockets of good practice, with social workers sometimes working against the odds. Sadly, the inspectors were often the first people to recognize the quality of this practice and to give encouragement. Too many social workers are 'heads down' in their own agency, absorbing the pressure, and are not encouraged to get 'heads up', to look around at how things can be different – there *are* agencies with good cultures and excellent practice. It is so important to maintain a broad and balanced perspective, as the authors suggest.

In common with the framework of this book, my own research for the Audit Commission and Department of Health in *People Need People** concluded that people are people, whatever the context, and that the same principles of good human relationships should be applied to the management of the organization as to the practice of social work. In fact, it can be demonstrated that organizations which uphold humanitarian values and treat their social workers in the way that they expect social workers to engage with the public are those most likely to have positive feedback from service users and a stable and positive staff group. In other words, social work values tend to support effective organizational performance and enhance the satisfaction of service users, a core message of this book.

* Joint Reviews (2000). London, Audit Commission, Department of Health and Office of the National Assembly for Wales.
www.education.gov.uk/publications/eOrderingDownload/JJR1453.pdf (Accessed on 25 August 2020)

The key principles of relationships, which have been affirmed in the literature about human relationships, human resource management, social work and many other sectors can be summarized as:

Fairness	or	**C**onsistency
Respect	or	**A**cceptance
Honesty	or	**I**ntegrity
Trustworthiness	or	**R**eliability
Understanding	or	**E**mpathy

This gives us yet another acronym – CAIRE – which puts INTEGRITY at the heart of CARE. We all have some scope for influencing the organizations we work in to implement these principles and to model the behaviours in our own daily work. The authors give helpful pointers to how each person can do this.

The Global Agenda for Social Work and Social Development completed its first decade in 2020; the final pillar focused on the importance of human relationships* in practice and in organizations. My long involvement in international social work, including four years as President of IFSW, showed me that the challenges described in this book are not unique to the United Kingdom. Indeed, one way and another they can be found universally. Despite the wide diversity of practice settings and economic environments found around the world, the basic challenge for social work of surviving and thriving in challenging environments is remarkably consistent. We are everywhere struggling with limited resources, challenging management environments and ethical complexities. This book is therefore helpful whatever the country or context in which you are working.

On a more personal note, I know from personal experience the truth in this book that feeling connected is energizing and creative. I am eternally grateful to my various employers who have supported my involvement in professional bodies. In fact, I am sure that I worked harder and more productively as a result of the stimulation I received from the few days committed to professional activity! I deplore those employers who obstruct and belittle professional engagement and obstruct social workers who aspire to be involved in professional associations. In my experience, involvement in professional

* Jones, D. N. (2020) *The Global Agenda for Social Work and Social Development. Fourth report: Strengthening the Importance of Human Relationships*, Rhinefelden, Switzerland, IFSW https://www.ifsw.org/product/books/global-agenda-for-social-work-and-social-development-4th-report/ (Accessed on 15 July 2020)

bodies is one of the most effective routes for continuous personal development, and for survival and thriving in social work and that it brings creativity and positivity to the agency.

So, finally, the key messages I have taken from this book, and which chime with my own experience, are that it is important to hold on to the humanitarian purpose and values which brought most of us into social work. Reflectivity is essential, for oneself and in discussion with others, to ensure that practice is purposeful and grounded in values. Relationships count. We must always include respect for others, whatever their circumstances. If we lose respect for the human dignity of others, we have lost our own moral purpose and self-respect. To keep to this realistic recipe for surviving and thriving in social work, it is also essential that we practise self-care, looking after our personal relationships and our own well-being.

It is difficult to live every day modelling respect for people, including respect for oneself, in challenging environments. It may be challenging but it *is* possible and realistic. The result, realistically within our grasp, is effective social work and self-respect.

David N. Jones
People Need People Consulting

Guide to further learning

As we have made clear, the subject matter of this book is immense, and so what we offer cannot be regarded as comprehensive or exhaustive – there is so much more that could be said about the issues involved. It is for this reason that we now offer a short guide to further learning. We want to encourage you to keep learning and thereby to keep increasing your ability to not only survive, but also to thrive.

We begin by highlighting three texts that we regard as essential reading, namely:

Collins, S. (2019) *The Positive Social Worker*, London, Routledge.

Ravalier, J. M. and Allen, R. (2020) *Social Worker Wellbeing and Working Conditions: Good Practice Toolkit*, Birmingham, BASW.

Thompson, N. (2019) *The Managing Stress Practice Manual*, Wrexham, Avenue Media Solutions.

Other texts worth exploring include:

Bloom, D. T. (2021) *Employee Empowerment,* New York, Routledge.
Costello, J. (2020) *Workplace Wellbeing: A Relational Approach*, London, Routledge.
Finch, E. and Aranda-Mena, G. (2020) *Creating Emotionally Intelligent Workspaces*, London, Routledge.
Friedman, R. (2014) *The Best Place to Work: The Art and Science of Creating an Extraordinary Workplace*, New York, Perigee.
Holloway, M. and Moss, B. (2010) *Spirituality and Social Work*, Basingstoke, Palgrave Macmillan.
Howe, D. (2008) *The Emotionally Intelligent Social Worker*, Basingstoke, Palgrave Macmillan.
Huq, R. A. (2015) *The Psychology of Employee Empowerment: Concepts, Critical Themes and a Framework for Implementation*, Farnham, Gower.
Monbiot, G. (2016) *How Did We Get into This Mess: Politics, Equality, Nature*, London, Verso.
Monbiot, G. (2018) *Out of the Wreckage: A New Politics for an Age of Crisis*, London, Verso.

Moss, B. and Thompson, N. (2020) *The Values-based Practice Manual*, Wrexham, Avenue Media Solutions.

Rosling, H. (2018) *Factfulness: Ten Reasons We're Wrong About the World – and Why Things are Better than You Think*, London, Hodder & Stoughton.

Thompson, N. (2018) *The Social Worker's Practice Manual*, Wrexham, Avenue Media Solutions.

Thompson, N. (2019) *Manifesto for Making a Difference: From Surviving to Thriving*, Wrexham, Avenue Media Solutions (downloadable for free from the Learning Zone at www.NeilThompson.info).

In addition, Neil has produced some relevant e-learning courses that are available at a discount to SWU members:

Dealing with Stress

Emotional Competence: Developing Emotional Intelligence and Resilience.

Handling Aggression

Time and Workload Management

(NB These courses are included in Neil's *Survive in Social Work* programme – see p. 216 below.)

The various resources highlighted in this guide are just a selection of what is available. So, whatever options you choose, we encourage you to make full use of them. The greater your knowledge of the issues involved, the stronger a position you will be in.

References

Albrecht, K. (2006) *Social Intelligence, the New Science of Success*, San Francisco, CA, Jossey-Bass.

Allcorn, S. (2005) *Organizational Dynamics and Intervention: Tools for Changing the Workplace*, London, M. E. Sharpe.

Atkinson, A. B. (2018) *Inequality: What Can Be Done?* Cambridge, MA, Harvard University Press.

Ballat, J. and Campling, P. (2011) *Intelligent Kindness: Reforming the Culture of Healthcare*, London, The Royal College of Psychiatrists.

BASW, Bath Spa University and SWU (2020) *Social Worker Wellbeing and Working Conditions: Good Practice Toolkit*, Birmingham, BASW.

Beck, U. (2000) *The Brave New World of Work*, Cambridge, Polity.

Billig, M. (2013) *Learn to Write Badly: How to Succeed in the Social Sciences*, Cambridge, Cambridge University Press.

Bolton, S. and Houlihan, M. (2007) *Searching for the Human in Human Resource Management: Theory, Practice and Workplace Contexts*, Basingstoke, Palgrave.

Bryson, A., Barth, E. and Dale-Olsen, H. (2013) 'The Effects of Organizational Change on Worker Well-being and the Moderating Role of Trade Unions', *Industrial and Labor Review*, 66(4).

Bunting, M. (2004) *Willing Slaves: How the Overwork Culture is Ruling Our Lives*, London, HarperCollins.

Calhoun, L. G. and Tedeschi, R. G. (2006) *Handbook of Traumatic Loss: Research and Practice,* New York: Psychology Press.

Cederström, C. and Spicer, A. (2015) *The Wellness Syndrome*, Cambridge, Polity.

Chang, H-J. (2010) *23 Things They Don't Tell You About Capitalism*, London, Penguin.

Chochinov, H. M. and Breitbart, W. (eds) (2009) *Handbook of Psychiatry in Palliative Care*, 2nd edn, New York, Oxford University Press.

Cole, B. and Pargament, K. I. (1999) 'Re-creating Your Life: A Spiritual/ Psychotherapeutic Intervention for People Diagnosed with Cancer', *Psycho-Oncology*, 8, pp. 395-407.

Collins, S. (2019) *The Positive Social Worker*, London, Routledge.

Cooper, J. (2015) 'Exhausted Social Workers on the Edge of Burnout but Still Achieving Positive Change', *Community Care,* July 15.

Corsini, R. (ed.) (1977) *Current Personality Theories*, Iasca, IL, F. E. Peacock.

Costello, J. (2020) *Workplace Wellbeing: A Relational Approach*, London, Routledge.

Coyne, J. C. and Tennen, H. (2010) 'Positive Psychology in Cancer Care: Bad Science, Exaggerated Claims, and Unproven Medicine', *Annals of Behavioral Medicine,* 39(1), pp. 16-26. doi:10.1007/s12160-009-9154-z

Crowell, S. (ed.) (2012) *The Cambridge Companion to Existentialism,* New York, Cambridge University Press.

Davies, J. (2012) *The Importance of Suffering: The Value and Meaning of Emotional Discontent*, London, Routledge.

Desai, S. (2018) 'Solution-focused Practice', in Thompson and Stepney (2018).

Dorling, D. (2011) *Injustice,* Bristol, Policy Press.

Dorling, D. (2018) *Peak Inequality: Britain's Ticking Time Bomb*, Bristol, Policy Press.

Dorling, D. (2019) *Inequality and the 1%*, 3rd edn, London, Verso.

Dreyfus, H. L. (2012) 'What a Monster Then is Man', in Crowell (2012).

Ehrenreich, B. (2009) *Smile or Die: How Positive Thinking Fooled America and the World*, London, Granta.

England, H. (1986) *Social Work as Art: Making Sense for Good Practice*, London, Allen & Unwin.

Fevre, R., Lewis, D., Robinson, R. and Jones, T. (2013) *Trouble at Work*, London, Bloomsbury.

Folkman, S. and Moskowitz, J. T. (2000) 'Positive Affect and the Other Side of Coping', *American Psychologist,* 55, pp. 647-54.

Gambles, R., Lewis, S. and Rapaport, R. (2006) *The Myth of Work-Life Balance: The Challenge of Our Times for Men, Women and Societies,* Chichester, John Wiley & Sons.

Gilbert, P. (2005) *Leadership: Being Effective and Remaining Human,* Lyme Regis, Russell House Publishing.

Gilbert, P. and Thompson, N. (2019) *Leadership: A Learning and Development Manual*, 2nd edn, Brighton, Pavilion.

Goddard, M., Mannion, R. and Smith, P. C. (2000) 'Enhancing Performance in Healthcare: A Theoretical Perspective on Agency and the Role of Information', *Health Economics*, 9, pp. 95-107.

Grint, K. (2005) *Leadership: Limits and Possibilities*, Basingstoke, Palgrave Macmillan.

Haile, G., Bryson, A. and White, M. (2015) 'Spillover Effects of Unionisation on Non-members' Wellbeing', *Labour Economics*, 35, pp. 108-22.

Ham, C. (2009) 'Lessons from the Past Decade for Future Health Reforms, *BMJ*, 339, b4372.

Hamer, M. (2007) *The Barefoot Helper: Mindfulness and Creativity in Social Work and the Helping Professions*, Lyme Regis, Russell House Publishing.

Hasson, G. and Butler, D. (2020) *Mental Health and Wellbeing in the Workplace: A Practical Guide for Employers and Employees*, North Mankato, MN, Capstone.

Hedges, C. (2009) *Empire of Illusion: The End of Literacy and the Triumph of Spectacle*, New York, Nation Books.

Howarth, J. and Hart, G. (eds) (2012) *Well-being: Individual, Community and Social Perspectives*, Basingstoke, Palgrave Macmillan.

Howe, D. (2008) *The Emotionally Intelligent Social Worker*, Basingstoke, Palgrave Macmillan.

Huq, R. A. (2015) *The Psychology of Employee Empowerment: Concepts, Critical Themes and a Framework for Implementation*, Farnham, Gower.

Iliffe, S. (2008) *From General Practice to Primary Care: The Industrialization of Family Medicine,* Oxford, Oxford University Press.

Illouz, E. (2012) *Why Love Hurts: A Sociological Explanation*, Cambridge, Polity.

Johnson, M. (2004) *The New Rules of Engagement: Life-Work Balance and Employee Commitment*, London, CIPD.

Jones, R. (2014) *The Story of Baby P: Setting the Record Straight*, Bristol, Policy Press.

Jordan, B. (2007) *Social Work and Well-being*, Lyme Regis, Russell House Publishing.

Jordan, B. (2008) *Welfare and Well-being: Social Value in Public Policy*, Bristol, The Policy Press.

Kent, M., Davis, M. C. and Reid, J. W. (eds) (2014) *The Resilience Handbook: Approaches to Stress and Trauma*, New York: Routledge.

Kinder, A., Hughes, R. and Cooper, C. L. (eds) (2008) *Employee Well-being Support: A Workplace Resource*, Chichester, John Wiley and Sons.

Kobasa, S. and Maddi, S. (1977) 'Existential Personality Theory', in Corsini (1977).

Kouzes, J. M and Posner, B. Z. (2007) *The Leadership Challenge*, 4th edn, San Francisco, CA, Jossey-Bass.

Lazarus, R. and Folkman, S. (1984) *Stress, Appraisal and Coping*, New York, Springer.

Liker, J. K. (2014) *The Toyota Way: 14 Management Principles from the World's Greatest Manufacturer*, New York, McGraw-Hill.

McFadden, P. (2016) *Measuring Burnout amongst UK Social Workers*, Belfast, QUB/Community Care.

Mendoza, K. (2015) *Austerity: The Demolition of the Welfare State and the Rise of the Zombie Economy,* Oxford, New Internationalist Publications.

Mickel, A. (2009) 'Survey Reveals Social Workers' Poor Working Conditions', *Community Care,* July 29.

Monbiot, G. (2016) *How Did We Get into This Mess: Politics, Equality, Nature,* London, Verso.

Monbiot, G. (2018) *Out of the Wreckage: A New Politics for an Age of Crisis,* London, Verso.

Mönnink, H. de (2017) *The Social Workers' Toolbox: Sustainable Multimethod Social Work*, London, Routledge.

Moss, B. and Thompson, N. (2019) *Spirituality, Meaning and Values: A Learning and Development Manual*, 2nd edn, Brighton, Pavilion.

Moss, B. and Thompson, N. (2020) *The Values-based Practice Manual*, Wrexham, Avenue Media Solutions.

Neimeyer, R. A., Pennebaker, J. W. and Dyke, J. G. van (2009) 'Narrative Medicine: Writing through Bereavement', in Chochinov and Breitbart (2009).

Ong, A. D., Bergeman, C. S., Biscontin, T. L. and Wallace, K. A. (2006) 'Psychological Resilience, Positive Emotions, and Successful Adaptation to Stress in Later Life', *Journal of Personality and Social Psychology*, 91, pp. 730-49.

Park, C. L. and Slattery, J. M. (2014) 'Resilience Interventions with a Focus on Meaning', in Kent *et al.* (2014).

Parker, J. and Doel, M. (eds) (2013) *Professional Social Work*, London, Sage.

Pickering, J. (2012) 'Well-being Local or Global? A Perspective from Ecopsychology', in Haworth and Hart (2012).

Pink, D. H. (2018) *Drive: The Surprising Truth about What Motivates Us,* Edinburgh, Canongate Books.

Ravalier, J. M. (2019) 'Psych-Social Working Conditions and Stress in UK Social Workers', *British Journal of Social Work,* 49, pp. 371-90.

Ravalier, J. M., McFadden, P., Boichat, P., Clabburn, O. and Moriarty, J. (2020) 'Social Worker Wellbeing: A Large Mixed-methods Study', *British Journal of Social Work*. ISSN 0045-3102 (forthcoming).

Robertson, I. and Tinline, G. (2008) 'Understanding and Improving Psychological

Well-being for Individual and Organisational Effectiveness', in Kinder *et al.* (2008).

Rosenblatt, P. C. (2020) 'Family Resilience in Dealing with Grief and Loss: A Sociological Perspective', in Thompson and Cox (2020).

Saleebey, D. (2012) *The Strengths Perspective in Social Work Practice*, 6th edn, New York, Pearson.

Sartre, J-P. (2000) *Huis Clos and other Plays: The Respectable Prostitute; Lucifer and the Lord,* London, Penguin.

Schneider, J. (2012) *Finding My Way: From Trauma to Transformation: The Journey through Loss and Grief*, Traverse City, MI, Seasons Press.

Schön, D. (1983) *The Reflective Practitioner*, Aldershot, Arena.

Schraer, R. (2015) 'Social Workers Too Stressed to Do their Job According to Survey', *Community Care*, January 15.

Scraton, P. (2016) *Hillsborough: The Truth*, 2nd edn, Edinburgh, Mainstream Publishing.

Smith, H. and Smith, M. K. (2008) *The Art of Helping Others: Being Around, Being There, Being Wise,* London, Jessica Kingsley Publishers.

Thompson, N. (2013a) *People Management*, Basingstoke, Palgrave Macmillan.

Thompson, N. (2013b) *Effective Teamwork,* an e-book published by Avenue Media Solutions.

Thompson, N. (2013c) 'The Emotionally Competent Professional', in Parker and Doel (2013).

Thompson, N. (2016a) *The Authentic Leader*, London, Palgrave.

Thompson, N. (2016b) *The Professional Social Worker: Meeting the Challenge*, 2nd edn, London, Palgrave.

Thompson, N. (2017a) *Social Problems and Social Justice*, London, Palgrave.

Thompson, N. (2017b) *Theorizing Practice*, 2nd edn, London, Palgrave.

Thompson, N. (2018a) *The Social Worker's Practice Manual*, Wrexham, Avenue Media Solutions.

Thompson, N. (2018b) *Applied Sociology*, New York, Routledge.

Thompson, N. (2018c) *Promoting Equality: Working with Diversity and Difference*, 4th edn, London, Palgrave.

Thompson, N. (2018d) 'Crisis Intervention', in Thompson and Stepney (2018).

Thompson, N. (2019a) *The Managing Stress Practice Manual*, Wrexham, Avenue Media Solutions.

Thompson, N. (2019b) *Tackling Bullying and Harassment in the Workplace: A*

Learning and Development Manual, 2nd edn, Brighton, Pavilion.

Thompson, N. (2019c) *Lessons for Living: 101 Top Tips for Optimal Well-being at Work and Beyond*, Wrexham, Avenue Media Solutions.

Thompson, N. (2019d) *The Learning from Practice Manual*, Wrexham, Avenue Media Solutions.

Thompson, N. (2020a) *Understanding Social Work: Preparing for Practice*, 5th edn, London, Red Globe Press.

Thompson, N. (2020b) *The Problems Solver's Practice Manual*, Wrexham, Avenue Media Solutions.

Thompson, N. (2021) *Anti-discriminatory Practice*, 7th edn, London, Red Globe Press.

Thompson, N. and Bates, J. (eds) (2009) *Promoting Workplace Well-being*, Basingstoke, Macmillan.

Thompson, N. and Cox, G. R. (eds) (2020) *Promoting Resilience: Responding to Adversity, Vulnerability and Loss*, New York, Routledge.

Thompson, N. and Stepney, P. (2018) *Social Work Theory and Methods: The Essentials*, New York, Routledge.

Thompson, S. (2019) *The Care of Older People Practice Manual*, Wrexham, Avenue Media Solutions.

Thompson, S. and Thompson, N. (2018) *The Critically Reflective Practitioner*, 2nd edn, London, Palgrave.

Tiberius, V. (2008) *The Reflective Life: Living Wisely with Our Limits*, Oxford, Oxford University Press.

Walsh, M. and Thompson, N. (2019) *Childhood Trauma and Recovery: A Child-centred Approach to Healing Early Years Abuse*, Brighton, Pavilion.

Walton, M. (2008) 'In Consideration of a Toxic Workplace: A Suitable Place for Treatment', in Kinder *et al.* (2008).

Waugh, C. E. (2014) 'The Regulatory Power of Positive emotions in Stress: A Temporal-Functional Approach', in Kent *et al.* (2014).

Waugh, C. E., Thompson, R. J. and Gottlib, I. H. (2011) 'Flexible Emotional Responsiveness in Trait Resilience', *Emotion*, 11, pp. 1059-67.

Welch, J. (2001) *Jack: What I've Learned Leading a Great Company and Great People*. London, Headline.

Westphal, M., Seivert, N. H. and Bonnano, G. A. (2010) 'Expressive Flexibility', *Emotion*, 10, pp. 92-100.

Wilkinson, R. and Pickett, K. (2010) *The Spirit Level: Why More Equal Societies*

Almost Always Do Better, London, Penguin.

Wilkinson, R. and Pickett, K. (2019) *The Inner Level: How More Equal Societies Reduce Stress, Restore Sanity and Improve Everyone's Well-being*. London, Penguin.

The Social Workers Union

The Social Workers Union (SWU) is a registered UK trade union for social work professionals and an organizational member of The British Association of Social Workers (BASW). SWU is devoted to social workers. Set up in June 2011, it was triggered by research among BASW members that indicated it was difficult to work under tremendous pressure to deliver social services and to be so often subjected to criticism in the media. Because SWU, unlike BASW, has a legal right for its advice and representation (A&R) officers to attend and represent at disciplinary and grievance procedures, SWU offers an extra layer of support to members.

SWU uses A&R officers who are also qualified social workers to advocate and negotiate on behalf of social workers, both individually and collectively, within the trade union movement and with employers. SWU offers guaranteed representation from a qualified social worker and is the only UK trade union for, and run by, qualified and registered social workers.

SWU is one of the fastest growing trade unions in the UK and is the only trade union to offer representation by a qualified social worker who understands the complexities of the profession. With officers working across the UK, we provide representation at internal hearings for disciplinary and grievance procedures, and employer investigations into practice and misconduct allegations.

The Social Workers Union, unlike a professional association, can guarantee the legal entitlement of representation in employers' hearings. SWU offers swift, practical representation and works with BASW which offers Advice and Representation (A&R) before the regulatory bodies. In these challenging times we believe that, working together, SWU and BASW provide the best protection and best advice for social workers from social workers.

SWU is an active member of the General Federation of Trade Unions (GFTU), providing our members with access to GFTU training. GFTU is a group of over 30 specialist unions with a combined membership of over 290,000. SWU has the additional strength of a large pool of union contacts in the workplace throughout the UK.

As well as providing support and representation to members at disciplinary or grievance procedures, SWU campaigns and lobbies on social work issues. The union has led campaigning on a number of significant campaigns, including Boot Out Austerity, Working Conditions Campaign, Austerity Action Group, the Ken Loach movie, *Sorry We Missed You* and the *SWU Social Work's Six-Point Action Plan*.

Also by Neil Thompson

Books

Neil has over 40 books to his name, including the following:

Social Work Theory and Methods: The Essentials (co-edited with Paul Stepney, Routledge, 2018)
The Social Worker's Practice Manual (Avenue Media Solutions, 2018)
Applied Sociology (Routledge, 2018)
Mental Health and Well-being: Alternatives to the Medical Model (Routledge, 2019)
The Managing Stress Practice Manual (Avenue Media Solutions, 2019)
Promoting Resilience: Responding to Adversity, Vulnerability and Loss (co-edited with Gerry Cox, Routledge, 2020)
The Problem Solver's Practice Manual (Avenue Media Solutions, 2020)
The Values-based Practice Manual (with Bernard Moss, Avenue Media Solutions, 2020)

E-courses

Neil has produced a range of e-courses, see below for details.

Learning Zone

Neil's *Learning Zone*, with free learning resources, is at:
www.NeilThompson.info.

Other Avenue Media Solutions Learning Resources

Avenue Media Solutions offers a range of learning resources:

Books and practice manuals | Training manuals | E-books | E-courses | DVDs

We also offer:

Survive in Social Work

An intensive development programme under the personal direction of Neil Thompson and geared towards helping social workers and managers to not only survive, but also thrive in today's difficult environment.

www.SurviveInSocialWork.com

Neil Thompson's Social Work Finishing School

An online learning programme for final-year students and NQSWs to help make the transition to fully fledged worker, plus an ideal refresher and re-energizer for experienced practitioners and managers.

www.SocialWorkFinishing.School

The Avenue Professional Development Programme

An online learning community based on principles of self-directed learning and geared towards developing critically reflective practice. Members support one another to take their learning forward as effectively as possible under Neil's guidance. **www.apdp.org.uk**

Practice manuals

Thompson, N. (2018) *The Social Worker's Practice Manual.*
Thompson, N. (2019) *The Learning from Practice Manual.*
Thompson, N. (2019) *The Managing Stress Practice Manual.*
Thompson, S. (2019) *The Care of Older People Practice Manual.*
Thompson, N. (2020) *The Problem Solver's Practice Manual.*
Moss, B. and Thompson, N. (2020) *The Values-based Practice Manual.*

In the pipeline:

Thompson, N. *The Loss and Grief Practice Manual.*
Moss, B, and Thompson, N. *The Spirituality and Religion Practice Manual.*

Other books

Thompson, N. (2019) *Lessons for Living: 101 Top Tips for Optimal Well-being at Work and Beyond.*
Thompson, S. (2019) *Your Social Work Journey: A Journal – From First Thoughts to First Placement.*

E-books

Mann, H. (2013) *Sleep and Sleep Disorders: A Brief Introduction.*
Mann, H. (2016) *The Cancer Challenge: Coping with Cancer When Someone You Love is Diagnosed.*
Thompson, N. (2012) *Effective Teamwork: How to Develop a Successful Team.*
Thompson, N. (2013) *Effective Writing.*
Thompson, N. (2015) *How to do Social Work.*
Thompson, N. (2016) *Tackling Bullying and Harassment in the Workplace.*
Thompson, N. (2016) *A Career in Social Work.*

E-learning courses

A wide range of cost-effective e-courses is available, including:

Dealing with Stress
Emotional Competence: Developing Emotional Intelligence and Resilience
Equality, Diversity and Social Justice
Essaycraft: How to Write Impressive Essays
Getting Started with Reflective Practice
Handling Aggression
Learning to Learn
Outcome-focused Practice
Risk Assessment and Management
Time and Workload Management

www.AvenueMediaSolutions.com

Printed in Poland
by Amazon Fulfillment
Poland Sp. z o.o., Wrocław

62091850R00125